Political Thought in Japanese Historical Writing: From *Kojiki* (712) to *Tokushi Yoron* (1712)

JOHN S. BROWNLEE

It was only at the onset of the Tokugawa period (1603-1868) that formal political thought emerged in Japan. Prior to that time Japanese scholars had concentrated, rather, on questions of legitimacy and authority in historical writing, producing a stream of works. Brownlee's illuminating study describes twenty of these important historical works commencing with *Kojiki* (712) and *Nihon Shoki* (720) and ending with *Tokushi Yoron* (1712) by Arai Hakuseki. Historical writing would cease to be the sole vehicle for political discussion in Japan in the seventeenth century as Chinese Confucian thought became dominant.

The author illustrates how the first works conceptualized history as imperial history and that subsequent scholars were unable to devise alternative schemes or patterns for history until Arai Hakuseki. Following the first histories, the central concern became the question of the relation of the Emperors to the new powers that arose. Brownlee examines the genre of Historical Tales and how it treated the Fujiwara Regents; the War Tales dealing with warriors at large, and specific works of historical argument depicting the Bakufu in relation to the Emperors. By interposing the works of *Gukanshō* (1219) by Jien, *Jinnō Shōtōki* (1339) by Kitabatake Chikafusa and *Tokushi Yoron* by Arai Hakuseki a clear pattern, demonstrating the sequential development of complexity and sophistication in handling the question, is revealed. Japanese political thought thus developed independently towards rationalism and secularism in early modern times.

John S. Brownlee is an associate professor of Japanese history at the University of Toronto.

Political Thought in Japanese Historical Writing

From *Kojiki* (712) to
Tokushi Yoron (1712)

JOHN S. BROWNLEE

Wilfrid Laurier University Press

[WLU]

Canadian Cataloguing in Publication Data

Brownlee, John S.
  Political thought in Japanese historical writing

Includes bibliographical references and index.
ISBN 978-0-88920-997-8 (hbk.).—ISBN 978-1-55458-450-5 (pbk.).—
ISBN 978-0-88920-874-2 (PDF).

1. Japan – History – To 1868 – Historiography.
2. Japan – Politics and government – To 1868 –
Historiography. I. Title.

DS871.5.B76 1991   952'.01'07202   C91-093963-2

⊗

Copyright 1991

WILFRID LAURIER UNIVERSITY PRESS
Waterloo, Ontario, Canada   N2L 3C5

Cover design by Leslie Macredie

Cover: Graphic adapted from flower and long-tailed bird (onaga-dori) pattern
  on silk fragment, mid-eighth century; Shōsō-in, Nara.

To Jill and Dean

CONTENTS

PREFACE

The major works of Japanese historical writing have been translated into English. Believing that these translations are made for the use of scholars, I have cited them freely; however, I have preferred my own renderings of some passages, as indicated in the footnotes.

Japanese names are given in Japanese style; that is, family name followed by personal name. For example, the name of Kitabatake Chikafusa gives first his family name, Kitabatake, and then his personal name, Chikafusa. The particle "no" has been eliminated from most names as unhelpful to readers of English (e.g., Sugawara no Michizane means "Michizane of the Sugawara family"; this becomes Sugawara Michizane, in the modern Japanese style). The only exceptions are the names of the men associated with the composition of *Kojiki*, Hieda no Are and Ō no Yasumaro, which are so familiar that they would seem strange without the particle.

The distinction between long and short vowels is preserved throughout the work by the customary macrons over "o" and "u" to indicate long vowels, except for the names of Tokyo, Kyoto, and Osaka, and the terms Shinto and Shogun which are familiar in English without macrons.

The research for this work has been conducted under generous grants from the Japan Society for the Promotion of Science, the University of Toronto, the University of Toronto-York University Joint Centre for Asia Pacific Studies, and the Social Sciences and Humanities Research Council of Canada.

This book has been published with the help of a grant from the Social Science Federation, using funds provided by the Social Sciences and Humanities Research Council of Canada.

I must acknowledge the assistance of many people. Kanai Madoka, Professor Emeritus, Tokyo University Historiographical Institute, provided a generous welcome to the Institute and arranged for access to the periodicals collection of Tokyo University. Ishida Ichirō, Professor Emeritus, Tōkai University, shared his many theories on Japanese history and society on several of my visits to Japan. Professor Kano Masanao, Waseda University, gave me much useful material and information. Professor Tamagake Hiroyuki, Tōhoku University, instructed me on Tokugawa period thought in a special one-person seminar. Hokao Ken'ichi, Professor Emeritus, Tōhoku University, arranged for me to stay there in 1982 and 1983, and was a genial host. Professor Uwayokote Masataka, who suffered through my first year as a Research Fellow at Kyoto University, has been unfailingly kind and helpful ever since.

The stern criticisms of Professor David Abosch of the State University of New York at Buffalo were most helpful. Professor James McMullen extended a timely invitation to Oxford University in 1985 to organize my thoughts. Mr. John Parry was an invaluable copy editor. The staff of the East Asian Library, University of Toronto, especially Mr. David Chang, were always helpful.

Finally, I must acknowledge the one who filled up my room with a rising pool of ink, so that I had either to write in order to diminish it, or drown.

Toronto, Canada
March 1, 1990   *J. S. B.*

古事記上卷 序并

臣安萬侶言夫混元既凝氣象未效無名無莊誰知其形然

乾坤初分參神作造化之首陰陽斯開二靈爲群品之祖

所以出入幽顯日月彰於洗目浮沈海水神祇呈於滌身

故太素杳冥因本教而識孕土產嶋之時元始綿邈頼先聖

而察生神立人之世寔知懸鏡吐珠而百王相續喫劔切蛇

以万神蕃息與議安河而平天下論小濱而清國土是以番

仁岐命初降于高千嶺神倭經歷于秋津嶋化熊出

The oldest manuscript of Japan's oldest book: the Shinpukuji text (1370) of *Kojiki* (712). (Courtesy of Shogakukan Inc., Tokyo.)

The gate of Fujimori Shrine, Kyoto. The principal deity is Prince Toneri, who presented *Nihon Shoki* to the throne in 720. Because "toneri" also meant the name of a low official in ancient times, the shrine pronounces the name of its deity "Iehito."

Retired Emperor Go Toba, who tried to overthrow the Kamakura Bakufu in the Jōkyū War, 1221, and failed. (Courtesy of Chikuma Shobō Publishing Company Ltd., Tokyo.)

The burial place of Emperor Chūkyō, atop a hill in Fushimi-ku, Kyoto; there are few visitors. He reigned as a child for 70-odd days in 1221, and was deposed after the Jōkyū War.

Myōe Shōnin of the Kegon Sect, in meditation in nature. His biography, *Myōe Shōnin Denki*, contains the sharpest political analysis in traditional Japanese history. (Courtesy of Kōdansha Ltd., Tokyo.)

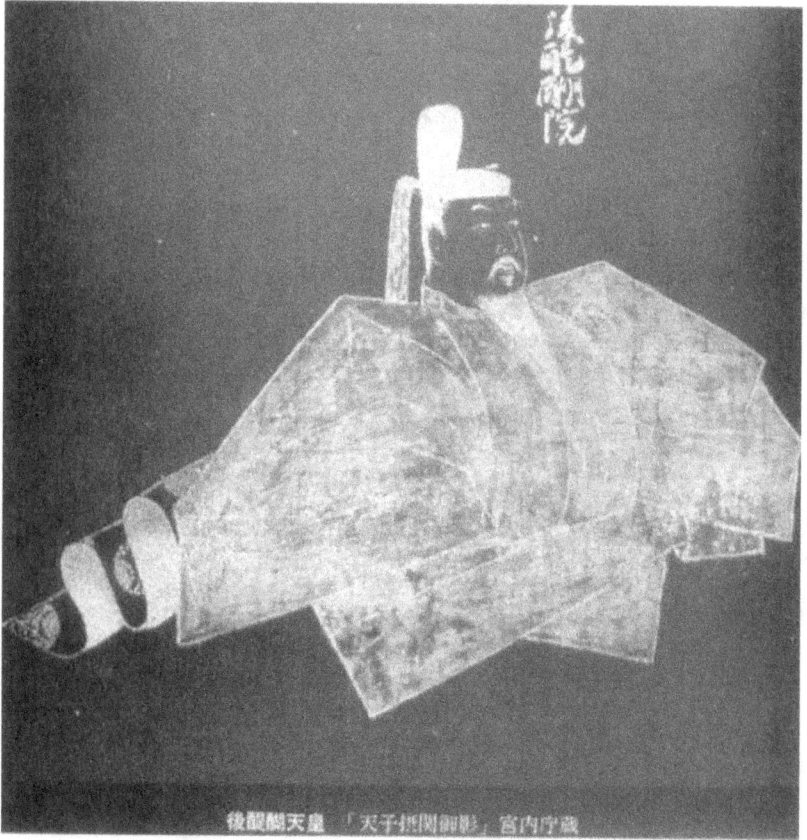

Emperor Go Daigo, who succeeded in overthrowing the Kamakura Bakufu in 1333.

Arai Hakuseki, author of the rationalist history *Tokushi Yoron* (1712). (Courtesy of Yoshikawa Kōbunkan, Tokyo.)

1940—A YEAR OF SINGULAR IMPORTANCE

The year 1940 was the 2,600th anniversary of the accession of the first Emperor of Japan, Emperor Jinmu in 660 B.C. The event was entirely mythical; yet, remarkably, the government of Japan was organized under a constitution of 1889 which accepted the event as historical. The unbroken succession of Emperors from Emperor Jinmu was the explicit basis for Japanese imperial sovereignty. His accession was recorded in two works of historical writing unrivaled in authority, *Kojiki* (Record of Ancient Matters, 712 A.D.), and *Nihon Shoki* (Chronicles of Japan, 720 A.D.). How these works came into being, and how they shaped Japanese thinking throughout history, is the main subject of this study.

It was one thing for the government of Japan to celebrate the anniversary of the mythical first Emperor; it was quite another for the historians of the day to acquiesce in the event. Scientific history entered Japan from the West in the late nineteenth century, and by 1940 it was clear to Japanese historians that the first histories, *Kojiki* and *Nihon Shoki*, were not authentic records of the past. Japanese historians knew very well that the story of Emperor Jinmu was a concoction made by unknown people, and recorded as fact in those two works. Yet none of the great historians of Japan spoke a word to that effect. A single scholar at Waseda University, Tsuda Sōkichi (1873-1961) had published works sceptical of the alleged facts of ancient history; for this he was brought to trial in 1941 on a charge of insulting the dignity of the imperial house.

There were many reasons why historians were silent upon the subject, chiefly the power of nationalism in a time of crisis, and the power of the

1

state to silence criticism of the basis of imperial sovereignty. In this work we turn to a third, the power of the tradition of Japanese political thought in historical writing.

INTRODUCTION

In the Japanese tradition there were no political philosophers before the Tokugawa period (1603-1868). This is surprising, because in earlier periods there appeared to be a need for some form of political expression. The first such era included the time of the establishment of the imperial state (550-700) and the period of its early maintenance (700-900). The second such era was the time of development and change; it included institutional and political change associated with the rise of the Fujiwara Regency (850-1185), and the wide-ranging challenge posed by the emergence to power of the warrior clans and the establishment in 1185 of a separate warrior government, the Kamakura Bakufu. The imperial government continued to exist after 1185, and antagonism between it and the Bakufu reached its height in a direct military confrontation in the Jōkyū War of 1221. The war did not resolve the political problem, and conflict continued throughout the Middle Ages, until by 1600 the warrior government came to dominate every aspect of Japanese existence. Then the problem faded into insignificance.

Neither era produced formal political writings. To some extent religion provided understanding, explanation, and legitimation, particularly in the era of founding the imperial state. To support its legitimacy, the imperial court exploited the religious beliefs of the country about the divine origins of Japan and the Japanese people. In the era of challenge, the Bakufu did the same thing but to a more limited extent, since the myths, specifically about the divine origin of the imperial family, could not be applied to the Bakufu.

The note to the Introduction is found on page 142.

3

It is not the case, however, that Japanese throughout history were unconcerned with the questions of legitimacy and authority that have engaged political thinkers in other societies. In the absence of discussion by philosophers or constitutional thinkers, political problems of Japan were in fact addressed by historians. This work shows how the historians tenaciously followed the vicissitudes of authority in Japan, and were particularly concerned with understanding and explaining the fate of the imperial house. According to their times and circumstances, historians took many different approaches to the problems, and we will discuss their diversity. At the same time, their continuing concern with intractable problems of the imperial house caused their thinking to develop into more complex and sophisticated modes, so that the story of Japanese historical writing is one of improvement and advancement. This is a story that has not been told, and it provides an unusual perspective on Japanese intellectual development. Yet it is not unreasonable to suggest that Japanese thinking changed and improved between ancient and modern times, when it was deeply affected successively by Chinese Confucianism and modern Western thought.

Emperor Tenmu, the most important figure in the founding of the imperial state, commanded the writing of *Kojiki* (Record of Ancient Matters, 712) and *Nihon Shoki* (Chronicle of Japan, 720). The ideas in these works, identifying the essence of Japan with the imperial house, had an overpowering effect on the Japanese consciousness for centuries. As the imperial court continued to flourish, the Emperors continued this practice and commissioned five more national histories: *Shoku Nihongi* (Chronicle of Japan Continued, 797), *Nihon Kōki* (Later Chronicle of Japan, 840), *Shoku Nihon Kōki* (Later Chronicle of Japan Continued, 869), *Nihon Montoku Tennō Jitsuroku* (Veritable Records of Emperor Montoku of Japan, 879), and *Nihon Sandai Jitsuroku* (Veritable Records of Three Reigns of Japan, 901).

In the era of development, the Fujiwara Regency presented a problem of intellectual accommodation: how could Japan have both an Emperor and a Regent? Historians addressed this problem in a new genre called *rekishi monogatari* (historical tales), most notably *Eiga Monogatari* (A Tale of Flowering Fortunes), *Ōkagami* (The Great Mirror), and *Imakagami* (Mirror of the Present Day), which were devoted almost exclusively to describing the splendours of the Fujiwara.

The later age of challenge posed by the rise of the warriors evoked a wider variety of responses in historical writing. First was the development of a new genre of *gunki monogatari* (war tales), which were politically unreflective and admiring works devoted to narrating warrior history. Like the earlier historical tales which glorified the aristocracy, these stories were produced in great numbers and encouraged unquestioning acceptance of the presence and the glory of the warriors.

The tremendous crisis of the Jōkyū War of 1221 provoked the second response, a work of political discussion unique in Japanese history: *Myōe Shōnin Denki* (Biography of Saint Myōe, mid-thirteenth century). It contains a sharp political discussion in which the Emperor is justified by a Chinese theory of absolute sovereignty; the Bakufu is shown to respond to this with a superior doctrine of good government as the justification of its power. Some historians responded to this discussion in *Masukagami* (The Clear Mirror, c. 1370) and *Baishōron* (Discourse of the Plums and Pines, mid-fourteenth century). They attempted to retain the theory of absolute imperial sovereignty, but had to recognize that subjects had in fact resisted the Emperor, so that their position was only hypothetical. With these two works, the issues raised by *Myōe Shōnin Denki* died.

Finally, the greatest works of Japanese political discussion contained in historical writing are three works of "historical argument" *(shiron)*: *Gukanshō* (Miscellany of Ignorant Views, 1219) by the high priest Jien (1155-1225); *Jinnō Shōtōki* (Record of the Legitimate Succession of the Divine Sovereigns, 1339) by Kitabatake Chikafusa (1283-1354); and *Tokushi Yoron* (A Reading of History, 1712) by Arai Hakuseki (1657-1725). Each was produced in response to drastically different conditions, but all addressed the central question of relations between the imperial institution and the Bakufu. The works were influenced by Buddhism, Shinto, and Confucianism respectively, but that does not explain their originality. The important thing about them is that the three in sequence show progressive development in complexity, sophistication, and credibility.

With the advent of Confucian philosophy in Japan in the Tokugawa period, the function of historical writing as the exclusive vehicle of political discussion came to an end. Men became conscious of the questions of the origins and purposes of the state in general, and laboured to understand the basis of the power of the Tokugawa Bakufu in particular. As we will discuss, the thought of Arai Hakuseki may be properly considered in this new context of Tokugawa Confucianism; yet his concern with old problems, approached from the point of view of a historian, justifies his inclusion in the group of works devoted to "historical argument."

Because traditional Japanese political thought is contained in historical writing, a special method is required to study it. Leo Strauss made a distinction between political philosophy, which is found in formal tracts, and political thought, which may be unorganized and expressed in numerous forms such as laws, codes, poems, stories, and speeches. Strauss says that whereas political philosophy seeks only knowledge, political thought "is indifferent to the distinction between opinion and knowledge." Further, political thought may be "the expounding or defence of a firmly held conviction or of an invigorating myth.''[1] This categorization applies to most of the works of Japanese historical writing. Therefore to elucidate them it is necessary to describe the historical circumstances of composition, the identity and affiliations of the authors, the sources, the methods of selection and presentation, and the apparent intentions of all the works.

With this in mind, let us turn to a study of the texts, beginning with *Kojiki* and *Nihon Shoki*. This method of analysis will show them to be superbly crafted works which fully met the needs of the society of the time for expression of political ideas.

PART I

CREATING IMPERIAL HISTORY

CHAPTER 1

Kojiki (712): Japan's First Book

Date and Authorship

The Preface of *Kojiki* says that Emperor Tenmu (r. 673-686) commanded a young man of prodigious memory named Hieda no Are, aged 28, to learn by heart certain texts of history. All these texts, whose titles indicate that they contained chronicles and genealogies of the imperial house and of the leading families, seem to have been lost by about the eighth century.

According to the Preface, Hieda no Are did as commanded and learned the texts, but nothing further materialized. No explanation is given for this lapse of activity. Emperor Tenmu died, and "the times went on and the reign changed before this was accomplished."[1] Empress Jitō (r. 690-697) and Emperor Monmu (r. 696-707) came and went, bringing to the throne Empress Genmei. She expressed concern at the state of historical knowledge: "Appalled at the mistakes in the *Ancient Words*, she determined to correct the corruptions in the *Records of Former Reigns*."[2]

Her remedy was to order a courtier by the name of Ō no Yasumaro, on the 18th of the ninth month of 711, "to record and present the *Ancient Words* learned by imperial command" by Hieda no Are.[3] Yasumaro reports that he complied despite the difficulties posed by the current condition of orthography, in which Chinese characters were still in process of being adapted to a variety of Japanese uses. He presented *Kojiki* to the throne in very short order, on the 28th of the first month of 712—just three months later.

Notes to Chapter 1 are found on pages 142-43.

The question of the author and date of *Kojiki* has given rise to much discussion among Japanese scholars. It is extremely important to them because of the traditional view that *Kojiki* was Japan's first book. Indeed, anything about *Kojiki* is important to them, because its ideas were the staple ingredients of the traditional Japanese world view, as we shall see. A survey of scholarship in 1977 by Tokumitsu Kyūya lists 60 publications on the date of composition of *Kojiki* from the 1940s to the early 1970s.[4] The flow of publications continues. However, despite an abundance of ingenious approaches, there is no clear consensus that *Kojiki* ought to be assigned a date of composition other than 712. Likewise, although strong doubt has been cast upon Hieda no Are and Ō no Yasumaro, no one else has been convincingly identified as the author. A review of scholarship on the subject is little to our point, since it is inconclusive. Instead, we shall accept the circumstances of composition substantially as stated in the book's Preface.[5]

Creating Imperial History

Kojiki is not just a transcription of the materials at hand in 712. The imperial state had a strong purpose in writing history: to establish an understanding of the past that would enhance its supremacy. Here is the command of Emperor Tenmu to Hieda no Are, which is recorded in the Preface to *Kojiki*:

> I hear that the *Imperial Chronicles* and *Basic Records* handed down by the various houses have come to differ from the truth and that many falsehoods have been added to them.
> If these errors are not remedied at this time, their meaning will be lost before many years have passed.
> This is the framework of the state, the great foundation of the imperial influence.
> Therefore, recording the *Imperial Chronicles* and examining the *Ancient Words*, discarding the mistaken and establishing the true, I desire to hand them on to later generations.[6]

The concern to establish an orthodox history, favourable to the imperial position, could not be expressed more clearly.

The impression is given that the memorizing done by Hieda no Are, and the transcribing done by Ō no Yasumaro, were both passive in nature. According to the Preface, their work consisted merely of accepting and passing on tales of the past. These tales may have been transmitted by specialists such as the hereditary guild of reciters (*katari-be*) and people with similar functions who were attached to the various clans. The impression that it was a passive recording is further enhanced by the contents of the work, which appear to be the natural beliefs of simple people of long ago. The tales of *Kojiki* are told with no sense of incongruity; the bad and disheartening stories about gods and Emperors are recited side by side with the good. For this reason Sakamoto Tarō has described them as "artless and childlike."[7] Although the stories certainly have meaning, the telling of them was apparently without concern for their political effects.

Nevertheless serious consideration must be given to *Kojiki* as a work of active scholarship. Emperor Tenmu noted problems in the existing works, and decided to "cut out falsehoods and establish the truth." The author of *Kojiki* did this corrective work on the sources, *Imperial Chronicles* and *Ancient Words*, and did it freely. Because of this reordering of the sources, modern scholars find it difficult to reconstruct the materials from *Imperial Chronicles* and *Ancient Words* that are contained in *Kojiki*. The phrasing of the Preface also alerts us to the active nature of the work, for the very words that Emperor Tenmu is said to have spoken were actually taken from a classical Chinese text.

The phrase "This is the framework of the state, the great foundation of the imperial influence," comes directly from the book *Wujing Zhengyi* (Orthodox Interpretation of the Five Classics), a Tang dynasty work compiled in 653 at the command of Emperor Tai Zong.[8] This shows that the author was well educated, knew Chinese sources, and was willing to borrow from them to fabricate an important part of the work, even taking the liberty of putting words into the mouth of the Emperor.

In the text as well as the Preface, the transfer of materials from Chinese sources can be readily observed. A striking example is the tale of Emperor Nintoku, the model of the benevolent Emperor:

> At this time the emperor climbed up a high mountain and, viewing the lands of the four quarters, said: "There is no smoke rising in the land. The entire land is impoverished. For a period of three years the people are released from all taxes and conscription."
>
> For this reason, the palace became dilapidated; although the rain leaked in everywhere, no repairs were made. The dripping rain was caught in vessels, and the inhabitants moved around to places where it did not leak.
>
> Later, when he viewed the land again, the entire land was filled with smoke.
>
> Therefore, realizing that the people were now rich, he reinstituted taxes and conscription.
>
> Thus his reign is praised as being the reign of a saintly ruler.[9]

Here materials from Chinese sources were copied down and passed off as the history of Japan.

Kojiki's version of Emperor Nintoku is merely an echo of the fuller story told in *Nihon Shoki*, which is rich with Chinese rhetoric. Without going into the question of which work, *Kojiki* or *Nihon Shoki*, influenced the other, or how they both drew upon other sources, we may safely conclude that Chinese sources helped the narrative history of Japan found in *Kojiki*.

However, it is difficult to proceed very far in describing what the author of *Kojiki* did to the materials at hand. The source works are not extant, so it is hard to reconstruct the ways the author copied, altered, selected, and edited his materials, and redistributed them over his narrative. There are internal clues to sources in the text of *Kojiki*, such as myth themes, word usages, place names, and so on, but only external sources could anchor sound interpretations.

Although one cannot easily reconstruct the process of dealing with the material, it is evident that the most significant accomplishment of the author of *Kojiki* was to create a structure for history. He devised categories for the material, and then arranged it in a convincing and apparently natural way. This was what made the work a success and a permanent source for the understanding of history by Japanese people. Perhaps the simplicity of the arrangement is its strength: *Kojiki* divides history into an Age of the Gods, and a directly succeeding Age of Human Emperors, beginning from Emperor Jinmu (r. 660-585 B.C.) and continuing to the end of the reign of Empress Suiko (d. 628 A.D.). Within this structure the materials were woven together. Let us examine some of the materials found in the myths of the Age of the Gods, and the tales of the Age of Human Emperors.

Myths of the Age of the Gods

If we view *Kojiki* as a work of political thought that launched the imperial state, we see that it rested upon a firm foundation of wider knowledge. The myths of the Age of the Gods were of fundamental cultural importance. In every society, culture provides answers to the basic questions of human life—who are the gods, whence came our land, who created humans, what accounts for collective agrarian life in indifferent or hostile nature, what becomes of us after we die? In addition, culture prescribes the moral behaviour that has permitted society to sustain itself. For the first time in Japanese history, *Kojiki* brought together the myths that answered these questions. More important, it tied them to the history of the imperial house, so that everything the Japanese believed in supported the concept of imperial sovereignty.

The Birth of the Gods

The first gods just "came into existence" (*nareru*). Then their population grew rapidly, in most extraordinary ways. Some were born by the same natural childbirth as humans. Some came from violent and putrid processes. For example, when the creator god Izanami died while giving birth to the Fire-god, deities came into existence from her vomit, faeces, and urine. Her husband Izanagi then killed his own child by cutting off its head; blood ran down the sword, and deities came into existence at each point on the sword where the blood flowed. From the body of the slain child there came into existence eight more deities: from his head, chest, belly, genitals, left hand, right hand, left foot, and right foot. These tales suggest a view of life as fundamentally abundant and end-lessly reproductive, by processes not to be closely analyzed. What was important was the overwhelming productivity of life, in which the posi-tive forces that generate life would always overcome the negative forces of death.

Another striking case is the descent of Izanami into the Land of the Dead. She is pursued there by the broken-hearted Izanagi, who violates the injunction not to look upon her. The body he loved is rotting and swarming with maggots, like any dead body ever observed on earth. Yet there are deities, or perhaps harpies, seen in her body in the same order as on the body of her slain child:

> Thereupon he broke off one of the large end-teeth of the comb he was wearing in his left hair-bunch, lit (it as) one fire, and entered in to see.
> At this time, maggots were squirming and roaring (in the corpse of Izanami-no-Mikoto).
> In her head was Great-Thunder;
> In her breast was Fire-Thunder;
> In her belly was Black-Thunder;
> In her genitals was Crack-Thunder;
> In her left hand was Young-Thunder;
> In her right hand was Earth-Thunder;
> In her left foot was Sounding-Thunder;
> In her right foot was Reclining-Thunder.
> Altogether there were eight thunder-deities.[10]

Repugnant as they may be, deities are everywhere, and command the interest and respect of humans. It is little wonder that Japanese viewed their country as a divine nation (*shinkoku*), a concept that would endure from ancient times to the twentieth century, and which affected the development of politics by inhibiting interference with the imperial house descended from the greatest deity, the Sun Goddess.

The Origin of the Islands of Japan

There are several stories about the origin of Japan; the most appealing is that of Izanami and Izanagi standing upon the Floating Bridge of Heaven. With a heavenly jewelled spear given to them by all the deities, they stirred the sea and lifted the spear; the water that dripped down coagulated and became an island. The other islands followed, some by natural childbirth of Izanami and Izanagi, until Japan as it was known was completed.[11]

Like the birth of the gods, the origin of Japan was essentially won-drous and pleasing to contemplate. These myths express an affirmative Japanese attitude towards their surroundings. The tendency to account for origins by known processes such as childbirth, without resort to metaphysics, may have a connection with their views of social and political processes. Essential political theory was also confined to affirming a known process, namely, the succession of Emperors. No attempt was made to measure politics by natural law or the rules set out by a deity. Thus the material presented *Kojiki* in the Age of the Gods is consistent with the principles of the Age of Human Emperors.

The Origin of Human Beings

Kojiki contains myths of the balance of nature and the beginnings of agriculture, and of the Land of the Dead, but they need not detain us here, since they have little direct connection with political thought. As for the story of the origin of human beings, there is none. They are part of nature, whose aspects are completely described in other myths.

This means that there was not much tendency in ancient Japanese thought to view society objectively. Human society was seen not as separated from its surroundings, but as entirely immersed in them and subject to their processes. This is connected with a lack of interest in objectifying rules of politics. Historical Japanese society did little to create external standards for itself, whether in the form of fundamental rules or of supreme beings who could direct, reward, and punish human beings. In the same way, many of the histories that we shall discuss, especially the Historical Tales and the War Tales, remained entirely within the boundaries of the institutions of their own times. They focused on the behaviour of individuals, without regard for the objective circumstances that influenced their actions. Those historians were like fish swimming, not aware of the water. This is consistent with the view of society presented in *Kojiki*. There is no sense of detachment from the surrounding natural environment, and no indication that humans are subject to different causes than other creatures. The myths of *Kojiki* do not recognize the existence of society as a major determinant of behaviour.

Conclusion

The placing of all this material into the Age of the Gods was natural for the author of *Kojiki*, since the myths came to hand in the form of tales of gods. We do not know how they were understood by the author—how old he thought the myths were, and where they came from. However, we can assume that they carried a certain inherent order and meaning, and that others besides the author had clear ideas about the sequence of events in history, so that his placement of materials in order was not entirely arbitrary. What is most significant is the active nature of scholarship in *Kojiki*. The truth about the past was put into an authoritative work, and a basic decision was made about the structure of history: there was an Age of the Gods, and then an Age of Human Emperors.

This decision could never be undone. People of later times forgot that the author of *Kojiki* divided history in this manner, and simply believed in the Age of the Gods and the Age of Human Emperors. Nobody disbelieved until Arai Hakuseki in the eighteenth century.

Tales of the Age of Human Emperors

When *Kojiki* moves from the Age of the Gods to the Age of Human Emperors, it passes from wide-ranging cultural ideas to more specific political ideas. Political ideas provided, first of all, a system of periodization for history.

There are many ways to divide history into periods. It may be done according to celestial bodies, or by the names of metals (Golden Age, Silver Age), or by the names of plants and animals. Nearly anything is possible. In Japan the decision was taken to divide the human portion of history into imperial reigns, and this was just as important as the decision to bifurcate all of history into divine and human sections. *Kojiki* tells the human history of Japan in terms of what happened during the reigns of 33 emperors from Emperor Jinmu to Empress Suiko. This was exactly the framework desired by Emperor Tenmu when he commanded the writing of the work. The general acceptance of this system in ancient Japanese society signified the ascendancy of the imperial house. No other family was important enough to devise a conceptual alternative for history.

Within this framework, events great and small are recorded, and a variety of purposes is served. The origin of the families of Japan is narrated, and they are placed into the context of imperial rule. The unification of Japan by conquest is told in a manner that both enhances the Emperor, and shows the loyalty and devotion of the great families to the Emperor. Japan's troublesome relations with Korea are presented, and reduced to a tale of mighty conquest designed to promote Japanese unity and pride. Let us survey some examples of each of these important categories of history.

The Origin of Families

As Emperor Jinmu travelled about, he encountered numerous persons of distinction:

> As they travelled on from there, a man with a tail came out of a well. There was a light in the well.
> The Emperor asked, "Who are you?"
> He replied: "I am an earthly deity. My name is Ihika" (the light in the well).
> This was the ancestor of the Obito of Yoshino.[12]

This is not an aimless story, told for the sake of interest. We do not know how important this encounter was for the man with the tail. However, we may surmise that the Obito, who had lately fallen into misfortune, were gratified to have their ancestry enhanced by being placed into the reign of the first Emperor. An ancient family of some prominence in pre-Taika Japan, they did not fare well after the Taika Reform of 645 which inaugurated the institutions of the Chinese-style state, and lost their place entirely in the 684 reform of titles by Emperor Tenmu. However, the family did survive into the Heian period, and the clan name reappears in the reign of Emperor Junna (r. 823-833).[13]

A great deal of space in *Kojiki* is used in this way to insert voluminous genealogical information. The records of the relatives of the Emperor, by blood and by marriage, were especially important; hence these accounts were extremely detailed. For example, the 10 Empresses or consorts of Emperor Ōjin (r. 270-31) are all named in full, along with their children, whose number totalled 27.[14] This kind of genealogical information was slanted towards satisfying the pride of existing families at the time of composition of *Kojiki*, as in the case of the Obito family. It was not necessarily accurate.

The Unification of Japan by Conquest

According to *Kojiki*, the unification of Japan by conquest was achieved mainly by Emperor Jinmu, the first human Emperor. One example of a campaign is the fight against the Earth-Spider People (*Tsuchi gumo*):

> When (Kamu-yamato-ipare-piko-no-mikoto) arrived at the great pit dwelling of OSAKA, there were eighty mighty men with tails, of the TUTI-GUMO, waiting inside the pit dwelling with great clamour.
>
> Then the child of the heavenly deities commanded that a banquet be given the eighty mighty men.
>
> To serve the eighty mighty men he assigned eighty food-servers, and had each of them wear a sword.
>
> He instructed the food servers, saying: "When you hear the song, then cut (them down)!"
>
> The song which was a signal for smiting the TUTI-GUMO was:
>
> Many people are in the large
> Pit dwelling of OSAKA.
> Even though many people are there,
> The gallant lads of the KUME,
> With their mallet-headed swords, with their stone mallets
> Will smite them relentlessly!
> The gallant lads of the KUME
> With their mallet-headed swords, with their stone mallets—
> Now is the time to smite them!
>
> As this song was sung, they drew their swords and smote them all to death at once.[15]

Such a tale of conquest makes an obvious contribution to the concept of imperial sovereignty, which it was the duty of *Kojiki* to promote. The song, however, shows the more subtle and skilful way in which the historian worked toward his purpose. This piece, known as the Song of Kume (*Kume Uta*), is one of the most famous songs of ancient times. Probably it was in the keeping of one of the hereditary guilds, the *Kume-be*. The early history of the guild is obscure, but probably they were the ancestors of the Kume clan, of which several branches are listed in the ninth-century work *Shinsen Shōjiroku* (New Compilation of the Register of Families). They seem also to have been in a subordinate relationship with the Ōtomo clan which flourished at the court in the post-Taika period. During the prosperity of the Ōtomo at the court, the Kume Song was performed at important occasions by the court musicians. It remains in the repertoire of court musicians to the present day.

The Kume Song is one of courage, gallantry, and faithfulness in battle. It was therefore appropriate for the Ōtomo clan, whose traditional association was with weaponry. Tsuchihashi Yutaka suggests that at one time it may have been performed by the Kume guild as an expression of its faithfulness to the Ōtomo family.[16] However, at the time of writing *Kojiki*, it had already been taken up at the national level, where it was used for ritual reassurance of the Emperor.

The song probably originated around the fourth century. By placing it in the reign of the first Emperor Jinmu, the author enhanced the importance of both the song and its guardians, the Ōtomo. This also improved the image of the Emperors, by portraying the first Emperor of Japan as calling forth a spontaneous expression of loyalty and commitment from the Kume group, in the dangerous and important work of subduing the Earth-Spider people.

To sum up, this tale of the unification of Japan by Emperor Jinmu aided the firm establishment of the concept of imperial sovereignty. In the late seventh century when *Kojiki* was in the process of composition, there probably existed memory of a time when other clans possessed equally good claims to pre-eminence. Therefore it was necessary to present the ascendancy of the Yamato line convincingly. The Kume Song helped by enhancing the martial image of Emperor Jinmu. It showed him as the model warrior, capable not only of smiting the Earth-Spider people, but also of commanding the loyalty and bravery of his faithful men in killing the fearsome enemy. The transposition of the song from the ritual level into the legend of Emperor Jinmu may not have been done by the compiler of *Kojiki*. However, the manipulation of the piece displays the characteristic unity of purpose and method that always enhanced the imperial dignity.

The Conquest of Korea

Japanese relations with Korea were an important cause of the development of Japanese civilization and the formation of the ancient state.

First, Korean people immigrated to Japan from at least the fourth century and became part of the Japanese people who emerged on the stage of world civilization between 550 and 700. Hirano Kunio distinguishes five waves of immigration from Korea into Japan, with the fourth and most important wave occurring in the seventh century. The kingdom of Paekche fell in 660, and refugees from all classes of people fled to Japan.[17] They were successfully integrated into Japanese society of all levels, contributing their skills in art, learning, and administration to the process of development that suddenly accelerated in Japan in the late seventh century.[18] Their presence is reflected in *Shinsen Shōjiroku*, a work on the origins of the great families of Japan that was produced for the court in 815. Of 1,182 families, 326, or slightly more than a fourth, were of foreign origin (Korean and Chinese).[19] For several centuries, Japan and Korea interacted at many levels—social, economic, military, cultural, and linguistic. Of all this, however, *Kojiki* has literally nothing to say. It treats the Korean kingdoms entirely as foreign countries, and it tries to show only the dominance of Japan because of the actions of its mighty and valorous Emperors.

The history of relations between ancient Japan and the Korean kingdoms has become a subject of more objective scholarly study, as the Japanese Empire which collapsed in 1945 recedes into the past and out of the memory of active historians. Now Japanese scholars are less prone to assume the superiority of Japan over Korea in ancient times, and are examining the role of foreign relations with Korea in the domestic history of Japan.[20] To sketch the picture quickly, Japan had a centuries-long involvement with the three Korean kingdoms of Silla (traditional founding date 57 B.C.), Paekche (traditional founding date 18 B.C.), and Koguryo (traditional founding date 37 B.C.). This was because of a Japanese claim to possession of territory called Imna, or Mimana, on the southernmost portion of the peninsula. The origin of this claim is obscure, but it is certain that it complicated relations with the three kingdoms, and led to sporadic Japanese military activity in Korea. There were ups and downs, some wins and some losses over the centuries, until the pace of events suddenly quickened in the seventh century and the outcome became decisive. The kingdom of Silla gained the upper hand, in alliance with Tang dynasty China, while Japan's allies, Paekche and Koguryo, proceeded towards defeat and extinction. Along the way to their extinction, Japanese naval forces suffered a resounding defeat at Hakusuki no E (Korean: Paekch'on-gang) in 663 at the hands of Silla and China. Silla finally unified the peninsula under its rule in 676. Thus the Japanese experience in the seventh century was one of loss and of menace. Fear of attack by Silla and China was one factor that stimulated the Japanese to undertake massive domestic reform, beginning with the Taika Reform of 645, and proceeding through several stages of legislation and construction, culminating in the Taihō Law codes of 701.

Japan's experience with Korea just prior to the writing of *Kojiki* was one of defeat and fear. What *Kojiki* did, however, was to reduce the time scale to the reigns of only two Emperors, Chūai (r. 192-200) and Empress Regent Jingū (r. 201-269), safely in the remote past. The actual existence of both of these rulers is open to doubt. In addition, it presented Japanese-Korean relations entirely from the point of view of Japan's conquest of a foreign land.

First, Emperor Chūai was advised by his divinely possessed Empress that Korea is a wealthy and desirable place. This Emperor did not make it to Korea, however. He disputed the divine claim, saying one could see no land, only the ocean. Then, "Saying [that this was] a deceiving deity, he pushed away the cither and sat silent without playing it."[21] Before they could restore the situation, he died.

Next, Empress Regent Jingū crossed to Korea with a mighty force; the Korean kings were so awe-struck that they placed themselves under her without fighting, becoming tributaries.[22] Beyond this, the narrative about Korea in *Kojiki* is confined to a notice of Korean immigration in the reigns of Emperor Ōjin (r. 270-310) and Emperor Yūryaku (r. 456-479), and the arrival of educated people, Confucian books, and artisans in the reign of Emperor Ōjin.

From *Nihon Shoki* we know that a great deal of historical information about Korea was available at the time *Kojiki* was compiled. *Kojiki*, however, sought to present Japanese-Korean relations in the same manner as the exploits of Emperor Jinmu. Flying in the face of real historical knowledge, *Kojiki* continued its steadfast purpose of glorifying the Emperors and of promoting national pride by depicting Japan as superior to Korea.

Acceptance of the Imperial Framework for History

Kojiki divided history into the Age of the Gods and the Age of Human Emperors, placing the myths of fundamental cultural importance in the Age of the Gods, and tales of early Japanese society in the Age of Human Emperors. In both cases, the materials were presented in a manner designed to enhance the Emperors. Creating a framework for historical thinking was just as important as making an authoritative record, and this was especially significant for the Age of Human Emperors. This framework of the succession of Emperors continued to be employed by all historical writing after *Kojiki*, beginning with *Nihon Shoki*.

In *Kojiki*, a way of thinking about history was established, in which facts would not make sense if there were no reigns of Emperors in which to place them. This may be seen in the following example.

In the centuries following completion of *Kojiki* and *Nihon Shoki*, there was a great deal of competition for place and property among the leading families of Japan, and they based their claims upon alleged facts of history. When seeking favours from the throne, they would recount the merits of their ancestors to strengthen their case. Thus we find that according to *Nihon Sandai Jitsuroku* (Veritable Records of Three Reigns of Japan), in 861 a certain Saeki Toyoo of Sanuki Province on Shikoku Island claimed to be a Saeki of a line directly descended from the Ōtomo clan (Saeki no Atai). His claim was supported by a prominent minister of state, Tomo Yoshio (811-868), who verified a brief history of the Saeki clan, stating that it was based on an examination of family records. In this Saeki family history, reference was made to ancestral affairs in the reigns of three Emperors: twelfth Emperor Keikō (r. 71-130), nineteenth Emperor Ingyō (r. 412-453), and thirty-sixth Emperor Kōtoku (r. 645-654).[23]

These ancestral affairs need not concern us, nor the validity of the claim, which is clearly questionable simply for employing the fabricated history of Japan. However, an historical claim of some importance was based on a concept of history involving the sequence of Emperors. Saeki Toyoo did not conceive of the history of his family in independent terms, or in relation to other families, but in terms of the reigns of Emperors. It was hardly an original approach; rather it was the universal understanding. In fact the claim was accepted; Saeki Toyoo received the rank of Sukune, which was the third highest, and was registered in the left (Sakyō) region of the capital. However, modern authorities emphatically state that the claim was not truthful.[24]

It is impossible to say whether the author of *Kojiki* constructed the imperial framework in detail, or whether the sequence of Emperors was already established at the time of composition. In either case, *Kojiki* imparted final authority to the imperial framework. Saeki Toyoo, and everyone else besides, accepted it without second thought and used it without noticing. For them, the imperial framework had become natural and true.

Emperor Tenmu had found historical knowledge in disorder, and he saw in this a threat to the foundation of the nation. If he had lived to see historical knowledge reorganized in *Kojiki*, he might well have been pleased, and content that the great foundation of the nation was secure.

CHAPTER 2

Nihon Shoki (720): The First National History

Date of Composition

The date of composition of *Nihon Shoki* is important because of the light it sheds on the stature of the work as a document of political thought. If it were begun in 681 by a team of princes and high officials and completed in 720, as the evidence suggests, two generations or more worked on the text. In those forty years, their collective skills as historians probably improved. More important, they probably found ways to make the imperial version of history acceptable to the leading families of the time. There is no evidence that anyone in 720 disputed the contents of *Nihon Shoki*; instead the textual and stylistic evidence suggests that the interests of the major families had been incorporated into the imperial history. If it were written over those forty years, it represents a consensus on the political ideas of Japan and becomes a document of overwhelming importance.

However, as with *Kojiki*, there are some problems regarding the date of composition. According to the most commonly held view, *Nihon Shoki* also arose from a command of Emperor Tenmu to compile a historical work. It seems that after commanding Hieda no Are to learn the materials that ultimately appeared in *Kojiki*, Emperor Tenmu gave separate orders in 681 for a different kind of historical compilation. However, it is difficult to trace the history of *Nihon Shoki* from its inception. This is because *Nihon Shoki* has no preface concerning its composition, authorship, and purpose. Probably there was originally a

Notes to Chapter 2 are found on page 143.

preface which has been lost, together with a book of genealogy that accompanied the work. They were included in the text, according to the account of the presentation of *Nihon Shoki* to the throne which is given in *Shoku Nihongi* (Chronicle of Japan Continued).[1] Such prefaces always gave a date of receiving the imperial command to compile the history, and without this essential information as a starting point, the discussion of the date of composition becomes more difficult.

The apparent origin of the work is recorded in an entry in the text of *Nihon Shoki* itself, in the year 681 (third month, sixteenth day):

> The Emperor took his place in the Great Hall of Audience, and there gave orders to the Imperial Princes Kahashima and Osakabe, to Prince Hirose, Prince Takeda, Prince Kuhada, and Prince Mino, to Michichi, Kamit-sukenu no Kimi, of Lower Daikin rank, and Kobito, Imbe no Muraji, of Middle Shokin rank, Inashiki, Adzumi no Muraji, of Lower Shokin rank, Ohagata, Naniha no Muraji, Ohoshima, Nakatomi no Muraji, of Upper Daisen rank, and Kobito Heguri no Omi, of Lower Daisen rank, to commit to writing a chronicle of the Emperors, and also of matters of high antiquity. Ohoshima and Kobito took the pen in hand themselves, and made notes.[2]

The command is clear, yet questions arise, as in the case of *Kojiki*. Why did Emperor Tenmu want two history projects? Was the order to Hieda no Are to correct the records and thereby produce *Kojiki* not sufficient? Since both books are histories of Japan, if the 680 starting date for *Kojiki* is taken as correct, would it not follow that the 681 starting date for *Nihon Shoki* is wrong?

The answer lies in the very different nature and style of the two works. They cover exactly the same period of history, beginning with the Age of the Gods and ending with the reign of Empress Suiko (592-628) in the case of *Kojiki*, and with Empress Jitō (r. 690-697) in the case of *Nihon Shoki*. Yet their differences in language, method, and emphasis are striking, because each work sought to fill a different need at the time. Separate assignments were necessary for His Majesty's history project because of the dual nature of the development of Japanese civilization.

On one hand, the rise of the Japanese state in East Asia required a local justification. Its founding by deities, and the record of its mighty and divine Emperors and great houses had to be told in *Kojiki*. Hence *Kojiki* concentrates on the early period, and narrates the Age of the Gods in considerable detail. Once past the era of the founding of Japan and the imperial house, however, *Kojiki* loses its strong sense of purpose. The narrative becomes thin for the later Emperors, and by the time Empress Suiko is discussed, *Kojiki* has nothing to say: it could not handle real history. Its emphasis on the period of founding was necessary in order to persuade other East Asians and the Japanese themselves that the Japanese were different and autonomous.

On the other hand, the means to the rise of Japan in East Asia, and its defence in the protracted troubles in Korea, were the adoption of Chinese institutions of government and culture. The accomplishment of the Japanese in this undertaking must have been a matter of great pride. By their own effort, between 550 and 700 they had established a more advanced governing system and had brought every region and family under its jurisdiction. Orderly government by literate officials proceeded under the guidance of law codes. Learning and culture were respected and pursued at the highest levels of society. The philosophically advanced religion of Buddhism was firmly planted on Japanese soil. At the end of the seventh century all these aspects of advanced civilization contributed to Japan's image as an autonomous and powerful empire in East Asia. This development also had to be displayed in *Nihon Shoki*, which was written appropriately in Classical Chinese, the language of high civilization in East Asia.

It is unlikely that Emperor Tenmu thought about the matter in this explicit way, reflecting on the need for a history of the time of founding, and for another history of the time of growth and development. Nevertheless, if Emperor Tenmu did actually command the two works, we must recognize the depth of his understanding of history. The ability to perceive both types of need, and to give precise directions for these history projects, required a genius of sorts. The same genius is evident in Emperor Tenmu's plan for establishing the concept of the imperial state, while skilfully devising methods for recognizing the importance of families. He stimulated them to work for the imperial cause, with several rounds of promotion in the 680s, and a complete reorganization of the court ranks in 684. This reform had the purpose of rewarding the supporters of the imperial cause and uniting them for further effort. As Ishida Ichirō points out, Emperor Tenmu used the energies of the old established families of Japan in creating a new state structure.[3] This ability to harness old forces in the service of a new system is related to his perception of a need for two works of history. *Kojiki* would fortify the sense of prestige held by the major families of Japan. *Nihon Shoki* would enhance the vision of the bureaucratic imperial state to which Emperor Tenmu was committed.

The date of *Nihon Shoki* also depends on the authors. Who were those people to whom Emperor Tenmu gave his command? Why were they so eager to begin that Ohoshima and Kobito "took the pen in hand themselves, and made notes"? Their court ranks were not high, but it appears that they were the winners in the long struggle to forward the imperial cause and reform in the Japanese state. The families named in this imperial audience, such as Kamitsukenu, Imbe, Azumi, and Nakatomi, apparently came to prominence after the Taika Reform of 645. This was the result of their service to the pre-imperial state. Powerful families of the pre-Taika era such as the Soga, Mononobe, Ōtomo, and Abe were not included among those who received the imperial command.[4]

It seems likely that the leading families of 681 were united in purpose after their great effort towards establishing firmly the imperial state. Nothing less than unity and common purpose can explain the swift completion of the law codes by 701, the establishment of governing offices in the capital and the provinces, and the building of the capital city of Nara from 710 onward. Probably this unity of purpose also affected the planning and writing of *Nihon Shoki*.

If we accept the view that *Nihon Shoki* began with Emperor Tenmu's imperial audience of 681, what about the 40 years that elapsed before it was done? A similar lapse occurred in the production of *Kojiki*; it remains unexplained. In the case of *Nihon Shoki* it is more likely that the work was carried on continuously. The project probably proved to be more difficult than anticipated. It was passed on to successors, and the scope of the project may have been enlarged. The preferred form and style may have become more apparent to those involved with it. For 40 years after 681 they carried out the compilation in circumstances new to Japan. That is, they lived under a freshly organized state, whose ruling elite was united and led by a vigorous Emperor. They enjoyed freedom from the anxiety and expense of the foreign crisis that had prevailed in the mid-seventh century. As they worked, they must have developed a better understanding of what it meant to compose of history of Japan. This process of developing a format would account for delay in production.

Except for a problematic command by Empress Genmei in 714 to two courtiers to "compile a national history," the project is lost to us again until 720. An entry in *Shoku Nihongi* says, "Prince Toneri, Imperial Prince of the First Grade, had previously been given an imperial command to compile *Chronicle of Japan*. On this date he completed the work and presented it to the throne. It consisted of thirty volumes, with one volume of genealogies."[5] We do not know how or why the project passed into the hands of Prince Toneri (676-735), but it seems that the long process begun in 681 had been completed at last. Apart from the loss of the preface and the book of genealogies, the work has apparently survived in its original form.

In summary, it may be concluded that *Nihon Shoki* was completed in 720, according to the entry in *Shoku Nihongi*, after 40 years of effort.[6] It was a major project of the state, and there was time and opportunity to develop a clear sense of purpose and to refine writing abilities. Kojima Noriyuki points out that *Nihon Shoki* displays an excellent grasp of Classical Chinese by its compilers, who were the best skilled among the scholar-bureaucrats and the naturalized immigrants of the day.[7] We should assume that there were many drafts during this long period of composition. We may also infer that some process of consultation went on with the great families of Japan, especially with regard to their views on genealogy. Although there is no direct evidence about such consultation, this inference is based on the certain knowledge that it was a joint composition, as demonstrated by the elaborate textual analysis of Kojima Noriyuki.[8] We conclude the same thing from the structure of the work, which skilfully integrates the history of the great families into the imperial narrative. Finally, the subsequent acceptance of the work by everyone as a true record of history indicates that all interests had been satisfied.

It is important not to draw the wrong conclusions from the fact that *Nihon Shoki* expressed the political consensus of the early eighth century. This consensus was not lying at hand, as it were, the natural product of society, just waiting to be copied down by someone. Rather it was the product of political effort, led by Emperor Tenmu, and of deliberate and careful work towards articulating the imperial ideology over a long period of time. This becomes clear as we examine the influence of Chinese models on the work and the system of dates developed in it.

The Chinese Models

China was an obvious source of political ideas for the Japanese of ancient times, since political philosophy had flourished there for a thousand years before the Japanese began to construct their imperial state in the seventh century. Confucianism, Legalism, Mohism, and Taoism all contained complete systems of political philosophy; and Chinese civilization in the seventh century carried forward an amalgam of ideas from these systems. Yet Chinese political philosophy held no direct appeal for the Japanese of ancient times, despite the fact that they modelled their government and laws after China. Instead of philosophy they turned to the Chinese histories for ideas and material to furnish the history of Japan. We are not certain why. It may be that Japanese thought in the seventh century was immature, and incapable of incorporating Chinese philosophy. This explanation is not very convincing, however, since later generations of Japanese displayed a similar lack of interest in Chinese philosophy. It was not until the seventeenth century, very late in Japanese history, that intellectuals took up Chinese philosophy.

More persuasive is the explanation that the Japanese perceived a lack of fit between Chinese ideas and Japanese political realities, although this is difficult to document. Chinese ideas justified the rise and fall of dynasties, as each rose in turn to claim the Mandate of Heaven, only to lose it to another. In Japan, there was only a single dynasty, started by the Sun Goddess, protected by her, and destined to endure forever. The contrast between the two systems was not clearly articulated until the eighteenth century, when the National Scholar Motoori Norinaga (1730-1801) vehemently denounced the Chinese political system, and argued that Chinese thought had no connection with the divinely protected Japanese system. To the extent that Japanese accepted Chinese ideas, said Norinaga, they brought untold harm to Japan. A person who seizes the throne, said he, is a thief and a robber; how could he ever be respected as a supreme ruler? Chinese thought that tried to persuade men to honour thieves and robbers was inherently trash and nonsense.[9] Such considerations may have influenced the Japanese of ancient times, although they did not articulate these ideas. What is certain is that, while they neglected philosophy, they relied heavily on Chinese historical writing when they composed the history of Japan in *Nihon Shoki*.

A rich collection of Chinese histories was at hand, which provided the models for *Nihon Shoki*. As we have noted, Chinese histories also affected the composition of *Kojiki*, but not to the extent of *Nihon Shoki*. *Kojiki* dealt primarily with myths and genealogies, seeking to present a unique view of Emperors descending in unbroken succession from deities and ruling by right of birth alone. This simple purpose of retailing myths was not well served by the model histories of China; thus *Kojiki* had no model. It stands alone. *Nihon Shoki*, however, went beyond the myths to deal with the documented history of Japan, and the Chinese model histories became extremely influential.

The Chinese histories were the product of an advanced civilization, with a highly developed bureaucratic system of imperial government. This was put into place centuries before Japan attempted historical writing. Japan had long been moving in the same direction of development towards a centralized bureaucratic empire, modelled precisely after China. In this historical context, it was natural for the scholars and officials assigned to the *Nihon Shoki* project to turn to the Chinese histories for models.

Chinese histories were first done by private scholars. The best surviving history from pre-Han times was the *Spring and Autumn Annals* (Chun Qiu), a chronicle compiled in the state of Liu, the home of Confucius. It covered events in the feudal states during the period 722-480 B.C., before the founding of the empire. Throughout most of Chinese history the work was ascribed to Confucius; this ascription was nothing more than a matter of faith, but it had the effect of enhancing the authority of the work. Equally respected as a source for the pre-imperial period is the *Commentary of Zuo* (Zuo Zhuan, *c.* third century B.C.) on the *Spring and Autumn Annals*. This work provides much additional narrative as well as commentary. As finished histories these two works are primitive, and for modern historians they have ceased to be historically accurate. However, they were firmly established as models of finished history books at the time *Nihon Shoki* was composed in the eighth century, and their annalistic form (*Bian-nian ti*; *hennentai* in Japanese) was adopted by *Nihon Shoki*. An example of this form:

1. In the (duke's) fifth year, in spring, in the first month, on Keah-seuh or Keach:ow, Paou, marquis of Ch'in, died.
2. In summer, the marquis of Ts'e and the earl of Ch'ing went to Ke.
3. The king (by) Heaven's (grace), sent the son of Jing Shuh to Loo with friendly inquiries.
4. There was the burial of duke Hwan of Ch'in.
5. We walled Chuh-k'ew.[10]

The *Commentary of Zuo* elaborates upon the bare facts, and makes history more vivid by providing a record of conversation and formal speeches of the historical actors. The fact that the speeches were often imaginary, and display formal literary style, did not lessen their influence on the formation of historiography in China and subsequently in Japan. They helped to enliven the narrative and provided emotional persuasion to support the argument of the work. However, the use of speech is somewhat unskilful in *Nihon Shoki*, occurring mainly in situations where Emperors made pronouncements on matters of government.

Although *Nihon Shoki* retained the form of annals established in the *Spring and Autumn Annals*, it also benefited from the materials and historiographical skills developed in later Chinese writing. A pioneering work, which remains a classic, is *Records of the Historian (Shiji)* by Sima Qian (145-90 B.C.). Its form, known as the Annals-biographies or Composite style (*Ji-zhuan ti*; *kidentai* in Japanese) set up the model for subsequent histories of dynasties. These dynastic histories became known as Standard Histories (*Zhengshi*; *seishi* in Japanese).

Records of the Historian was nothing less than a history of China up to the time of writing. For an annalist, such a history would be a daunting project. Making a chronicle of the world year by year is manageable only by omission of material, but incompleteness because of omission violates the intention of annalism. Hence the author abandoned the annalistic style and made categories that permitted meaningful selection of facts, allowing for analysis and discussion. The style invented by Sima Qian consists of five divisions into Basic Annals, Chronological Tables, Treatises (e.g., ritual, music, calendar, astronomy, sacrifices, rivers and canals, etc.), Hereditary House, and Biographies. This form of writing permitted a much more complex and subtle handling of the materials of history than annals. In addition, the literary skill of the author created compelling portraits of people, which move readers to the present day.

Sima Qian was followed by another outstanding private scholar, Ban Gu (39-92 A.D.), whose *History of the Former Han Dynasty* was important in reducing the proper work of the historian to a single dynasty.

Great reinforcement was given when the state became involved in the production of histories. With Ban Gu ended the role of the single private scholar in producing a major history of the empire. The Han Emperors began to take an interest in history, and this marked a turning-point in the development of historiography in China. In the period between the Han and the Tang dynasties there developed the idea of an independent branch of government set up to write history. In the Tang dynasty, the Bureau of Historiography became fully developed "as a kind of permanent imperial commission, independent of any of the main divisions of the court or government."[11] It was especially productive of the history of dynasties, and the Tang dynasty produced seven in all. Thus the work of writing history became fully formalized.

Subsequently the concept of the dynastic history became deeply rooted, and the works came to be known formally as the Standard Histories. More Standard Histories were written with the passage of time, so that the number of works in the corpus varies according to the historical period under review. Following the Tang period, in the Southern Song dynasty (1127-1279), 17 histories were defined as belonging to the Standard Histories. In the Qing period (1644-1912) the number reached 24. In the Republic of China, the number was increased to 25 by the addition of a work on the Yuan dynasty (1280-1368) and to 26 by the completion in 1962 of a work on the Qing dynasty. This remarkable historical interest sustained over many centuries is a distinguishing feature of Chinese civilization. It is not surprising that the Japanese found it worthy of emulation in ancient times.

Thus the compilers of *Nihon Shoki* had the benefit of a large body of historical writing from China. Fifteen Standard Histories had been written by the time it was decided to compose a history of Japan, and while we cannot show that every work was to be found in Japan, the tradition exerted a strong influence on Japanese historical thinking.

The concept of the imperially sponsored history, represented by the Standard Histories, was the one adopted by the writers of *Nihon Shoki*. However, *Nihon Shoki* differed from the Standard Histories of China in two respects. First, despite being closer in conception and purpose to the Standard Histories, *Nihon Shoki* adopted the annalistic form found in the earlier works such as the *Spring and Autumn Annals* and the *Commentary of Zuo*. Perhaps this was because it was the first attempt in Japan, and historians were not skilled enough to go beyond the annalistic method. Second, in Japan a branch of government similar to the Bureau of Historiography in Tang dynasty China did not develop. As we have seen, both *Kojiki* and *Nihon Shoki* arose from commands to specific persons to perform a task. No institutional basis was provided for their work. Instead, we lose sight of both projects between the time they were ordered and the time of appearance of a work, which we believe to be the intended product. Histories subsequent to *Nihon Shoki* were produced in the same fashion: an imperial command was given to certain individuals, not necessarily historians, and they were somehow expected to produce the desired work. This was the method for the five major works that followed the format of *Nihon Shoki*, which carried the narrative of Japan from *Nihon Shoki*'s end date of 697 up to 887. These five works form a corpus known as the Five National Histories (*Gokokushi*). When considered together with *Nihon Shoki*, they become the Six National Histories (*Rikkokushi*).

The direct influence of Chinese historical writing on Japanese works lessened significantly after *Nihon Shoki* and its successors. Nevertheless, throughout the whole history of Japan, the form of historical writing retained the influence of Chinese tradition.

The other major influence of the Chinese histories, and also of works of literature, was on the contents of *Nihon Shoki*. It is apparent from the most cursory reading that events and speeches have been transferred from Chinese sources and incorporated into *Nihon Shoki* as the history of Japan. We noted this in the case of Emperor Nintoku in *Kojiki*. There are many passages of this type in *Nihon Shoki*; one example will be enough.

Emperor Jinmu makes a conquering expedition eastward across the land and then pauses to declare his intention "to make a vast and spacious capital, and plan it great and strong."

> At present things are in a crude and obscure condition, and the people's minds are unsophisticated. Their manners are simply what is customary. Now if a great man were to establish laws, justice could not fail to flourish. And even if some gain should accrue to the people, in what way would this interfere with the Sage's action? Moreover, it will be well to open up and clear the mountains and forests, and to construct a palace. Then I may reverently assume the Precious Dignity, and so give peace to my good subjects. Above, I should then respond to the kindness of the Heavenly Powers in granting me the Kingdom, and below, I should extend the line of the Imperial descendant and foster rightmindedness. Thereafter the capital may be extended so as to embrace all the six cardinal points, and the eight cords may be covered so as to form a roof. Will this not be well?[12]

All of this comes directly from Chinese sources. The modern editors of *Nihon Shoki* identify *Wen Xuan*, a sixth-century literary anthology, as the source of the general sentiment of the speech. In addition they cite seven points of the speech as derived from *Wen Xuan*, and one part respectively from each of *Zhou Yi*, *Li Jhi*, and *Huai Nan Zi*.[13]

It is unlikely that this Chinese speech of Emperor Jinmu lay at hand somewhere in tradition. It is far too literary for that. The conclusion is inescapable that the compilers of *Nihon Shoki* deliberately falsified history to glorify Japan and the Emperors. We have seen that *Kojiki* did this too, for example in its handling of Japanese-Korean relations. One wonders what they thought they were doing. The first rule for modern historians, after all, is not to make it up. But this did not apply to the Japanese historians of ancient times. Keeping in mind that there was no distinction between myth and history, and no philosophical tradition to guard distinctions between truth and falsehood in general, we may understand these blatant concoctions as merely a practical attitude towards the task of history-writing. The compilers' purpose of legitimizing the Emperors was so strong that no means were considered unacceptable.

This attitude towards truth in history was not confined to the writers of *Kojiki* and *Nihon Shoki*. Remember that Emperor Tenmu commanded the writing of *Kojiki* in order to counteract the inventions and falsehoods of others, which were perceived to be everywhere. Fabricated history was particularly important for families hoping to improve their status; we have already seen the case of Saeki Toyoo, who made up his family history and had it verified by a high official. This was so common that the government took frequent and despairing note of it, and in 815 it tried to correct family histories with an authoritative work on genealogy, *Shinsen Shōjiroku*. The prefatory Memorial of the work complained about the way families of low status falsified their history: "They lie about their great-grandparents and they falsify their grandparents. They freely embellish their genealogy. They show proof that they are descended from deities and cite imperial origins. They falsely claim the right to wear ceremonial head-dress."[14]

One wonders whether any truth at all remains in the genealogical records of ancient Japan, and if so, how it can be distinguished from falsehood. This, however, is not our problem. We merely conclude that common standards of historical truth were so weak that the compilers of *Nihon Shoki* probably felt no intellectual discomfort at all when they copied down Chinese material as the history of Japan. Moreover, even as they perceived a sea of untruth all about them, they undoubtedly held a conviction that their own construction was true. Certainly that was the attitude of Emperor Tenmu.[15]

System of Dates in History

The most important achievement of *Kojiki* and *Nihon Shoki* was to establish the imperial reigns as the framework for history. Everything that had happened in history was slotted into a reign. Then *Nihon Shoki* took another step in establishing the imperial framework by assigning dates to historical events. This was the direct result of adopting the Chinese annalistic form, which gave the date of events. The simple expedient of dating events gave greater authority to this work of history by giving an impression of exactness. It is only an impression; the compilers of *Nihon Shoki* had to invent its dates. However, this was not recognized: throughout Japanese history up to the twentieth century, the dates given in *Nihon Shoki* were accepted as authentic.

History as known to the compilers of *Nihon Shoki* must not have appeared as a sequence of events stretched upon a linear time chart. For the princes, courtiers, and scholars who were set to work by the command of Emperor Tenmu, there was a great mass of information to be sorted out, and many of the stories at hand probably carried few clues about when the events had taken place. Therefore it was up to the compilers to make major decisions about the material, assigning some to earlier periods and some to later. Then it was necessary to date it according to its apparent sequence. Where the sequence was not apparent, something else had to be done. It was necessary to assign dates arbitrarily to events, according to calendrical systems in use in the times of the compilers.

This necessity to assign dates required nothing less than the audacious act of regulating the dates of the Emperors' reigns. In *Kojiki* the core of history, when there was nothing else to say, was the sequence of Emperors. To keep the story going, it just listed them. But *Kojiki* did not attempt a precise chronology. The compilers of *Nihon Shoki*, working by the model of the Chinese histories, had no choice but to proceed to the next stage. They had to write a list of the Emperors in sequence, and say when each one had reigned. Manufacture was in order.

Somehow *Kojiki* and *Nihon Shoki* agreed upon the same list of names of Emperors; we do not know when or how this list was firmly established. Of course the portion of the list that extended backward for a few centuries from their own times was a matter of real historical knowledge, but the names and sequence of the first 15 or 20 Emperors were determined in a manner now lost to us. At any rate, with the list agreed upon, the compilers of *Nihon Shoki* assigned reign dates for the rulers up to Empress Jitō. This list is given in Appendix A; needless to say, the ancients did not think in terms of B.C. and A.D., but the whole discussion has been converted into the Western chronological system by modern Japanese scholars.

Trouble in the list is immediately apparent to the critical eye. First, these people lived too long. Emperor Jinmu reigned for 76 years, and lived to the age of 127 according to *Nihon Shoki*, and to 137 according to *Kojiki*. He was the first Emperor, but not the champion in this respect: the longest reign was by the sixth Emperor Kōan, who reigned for 102 years, and lived to 137 according to *Nihon Shoki*, or 123 according to *Kojiki*.

Such long lives are not uncommon in myth, however. Great forefathers in many societies were expected to exhibit some unusual quality of this type, and before modern times no one was troubled about the extraordinary longevity of Japanese Emperors. In a similar way, Christians throughout history, whose life-span was fixed at 70 years by holy scripture, were not worried about the age of Methuselah, who lived for

969 years according to the same scripture. However, the acceptance of such a discrepancy is more difficult among the ordinary educated populace of modern times, and cannot survive the critical scrutiny of scholars at all. Such discrepancies only serve to alert scholars to peculiarities of the work.

Second, the lists of Emperors found in both *Kojiki* and *Nihon Shoki* disagree on the ages of the Emperors. *Kojiki* gives the age at death of 24 of the 33 Emperors whom it discusses. But the age agrees with that given in *Nihon Shoki* in only two cases: the 14th Emperor Chūai, who lived to 52, and his successor the Empress Regent Jingū, who lived to 100.[16] Which work should the reader believe?

Third, there are internal contradictions in the dates given in *Nihon Shoki*. For example, calculation based on the information given shows that Emperor Chūai was born 35 years after the death of his father[17]—a long pregnancy, inspiring sympathy for the mother.

The method by which the compilers of *Nihon Shoki* arrived at their chronology is known. Among the ideas then current was a complex set of notions related to the cyclical nature of time. This is known as the interpretation of astronomical phenomena as causation of earthly matters (*shin'i setsu*). The fundamental period is a complete cycle of 60 years, in which the years are named, and the names bear a deep significance. The year 601, the ninth year of the reign of Empress Suiko, was a year called *kanototori*, important as one of great change, or revolution (*kakumei*). It was not necessary to the calculation of time to observe the actual occurrence of great change in that year; it was only important to know that it had such a meaning. Then the year 601 provided a basis from which to calculate backwards into the timeless past. They were trying to find the date for the year when something important occurred, namely, the accession of Jinmu, the first Emperor of Japan.

The most auspicious method of figuring on the basis of 601 was the use of another cycle, consisting of the fundamental cycle of 60 years, taken 21 times. A year in the cycle which is 21 times 60 is called *ippō* and is a time of great change. Thus the compilers of *Nihon Shoki* calculated backwards from 601 for 21 times 60 years, or 1,260 years, and arrived at 660 B.C. for the *ippō*, which had to be the year of the accession of Emperor Jinmu.[18]

After the whole amount of time had been calculated in this manner, and the number of Emperors agreed upon, they were able to proceed with the distribution of the Emperors over the period. No doubt similar calendrical consideration influenced their decisions about the length of reign of the individual Emperors.

It would serve no purpose for us to try and establish a correct chronology. However, in looking at the way this chronology has been accepted, we note that the most important aspect was the determination to understand the history of Japan in terms of the reigns of Emperors. The accession of Jinmu in 660 B.C. became an established truth, which no historian in traditional Japan would ever have thought of questioning. Instead, the accession of Jinmu provided the way of conceiving of the passage of time.

The method of reckoning time from the accession of Emperor Jinmu even continued into the twentieth century as a clear and coherent dating system. It was useful in practice and had greater significance for Japanese than a system anchored upon the birth date of Jesus Christ. Some Japanese scholars before World War II, eager to uphold their nation's values, reckoned history in terms of the absolute number of years from Emperor Jinmu. For example, Nakamura Naokatsu used it in his biography of Kitabatake Chikafusa (1293-1354 A.D.), written in 1937 A.D. He gave Kitabatake's dates as 1953-2014. And Kitabatake's son Akiiye lived from 1978 to 1998, ancient Japan time.[19]

It is difficult to overestimate the importance of the dating system adopted by the compilers of *Nihon Shoki*. By giving an impression of scholarly exactitude, the dates lent credibility to the work. It also gave the Japanese a way of reckoning time on the basis of events that they alone understood.

CHAPTER 3

The Five National Histories and Imperial Scholarship

Historical Writing and Culture

The completion of *Nihon Shoki* was an event of great importance in the history of Japan. First, it marked the end of the interlocked processes of creating the state, and of explaining and justifying its origins: both the state and its history were universally acceptable in 720. Little more needed to be done, except to keep up with changing times. In politics this meant making adjustments to the system on a pragmatic basis, without reference to the Chinese blueprints for government. In historical writing it meant keeping the story up to date, without having to create concepts to express the history of Japan.

Second, the compilation affirmed the cultural character of the ancient Japanese state. At the highest level, that of the Emperor, cultural leadership was given by both example and command. The Emperors themselves wrote poetry, played, and sang music, not out of dissolution or a desire for diversion, but in the belief that such activities were an essential component of good government. Emperor Saga (r. 809-823) said, ''Nothing is greater than literature as a means of administering the state and governing one's house.''[1]

Third, the completion of *Nihon Shoki* signaled the exact nature of the cultural activities of the state. While a portion of these would consist of imaginative arts such as literature, another portion would be high-minded and serious scholarship. This was manifested by the periodic

Notes to Chapter 3 are found on pages 143-44.

readings of *Nihon Shoki* held throughout the Nara and Heian periods, and by the continuation of state-sponsored official histories.

There are records of seven readings of *Nihon Shoki* (*Doku Nihongi*), in 721, 772, 812, 843, 878, 904, and 965. Occurring at approximately 30-year intervals in the ninth century, they were intended to keep fresh the knowledge of *Nihon Shoki* in each new generation of courtiers and scholars. This was necessary to maintain the fundamental political knowledge contained in the work, and so retain a sense of the purpose of the imperial state. Another reason for *Nihon Shoki* readings was that the text itself was difficult. We have already noted Kojima Noriyuki's conclusion that the Chinese style was a composite one, reflecting the labour of many authors. Its peculiar literary competence was the work of the most skilled scholar-bureaucrats and naturalized immigrants of the age, who brought to bear their own "use of Chinese phrases, practical exegesis, employment of characters, idioms, and so on."[2] Hence serious study was needed for comprehension of this historical piece. In addition, the specific customs and appurtenances of ancient times required explanation.[3]

This record of *Nihon Shoki* readings illuminates the scholarly attitudes and methods of the ancient court. There are no records regarding the histories written after *Nihon Shoki*; literally nothing exists to show how official historical scholarship was done in the eighth and ninth centuries. But from the records of the *Nihon Shoki* readings we learn the collective nature of scholarship, involving the Emperor and the top courtiers. They were deeply serious about history, and they paid attention to accuracy and comprehension of the smallest details. These features made the histories they produced into sound and reliable works. They are still the first source of reference for modern historians of ancient Japan.

Composition and Methods

In all, five national histories were written in the era of the imperial court. However, when discussed in a context that includes the first national history, *Nihon Shoki*, they are collectively referred to as the Six National Histories (*Rikkokushi*). There has been little discussion in English of the Five National Histories. Moreover, the major English article on the subject—G. W. Robinson, "Early Japanese Chronicles: The Six National Histories," in W. G. Beasley and E. G. Pulleyblank, eds., *Historians of China and Japan* (Oxford University Press, 1961)— is unsympathetic, so a longer treatment is in order here.

The Five National Histories came about in much the same way as *Nihon Shoki*. From time to time there arose in this studious court a conviction that it was necessary to bring the record up to date. This resulted in an imperial command to specific persons to compile the history of a defined period. Again in the manner of *Nihon Shoki*, the task would be undertaken, only to lapse after a few years, necessitating a renewed command and the addition of more scholars to the editorial team. This was the case with *Shoku Nihongi*, the successor to *Nihon Shoki*: it was ordered by Emperor Kōnin (r. 770-781) to be compiled under the leadership of Ishikawa Nataru (728-788), Kamitsukenu Ōkawa, Ōmi Mifune (722-785), and Taima Nagatsugu. They produced a manuscript but did not finish the task, so their work to date was edited by a fresh team appointed by the next Emperor, Kanmu. It consisted of Fujiwara Tsugutada (727-796), Sugano Mamichi, and Akishino Yasundo. Finally in 797 the book was completed shortly after the death of the chief editor Fujiwara Tsugutada.

FIVE NATIONAL HISTORIES

Title	Date of completion	Period covered
Shoku Nihongi (Chronicle of Japan Continued)	797	697-791
Nihon Kōki (Later Chronicle of Japan)	840	792-833
Shoku Nihon Kōki (Later Chronicle of Japan Continued)	869	833-850
Nihon Montoku Tennō Jitsuroku (Veritable Records of Emperor Montoku of Japan)	879	850-858
Nihon Sandai Jitsuroku (Veritable Records of Three Reigns of Japan)	901	859-887

Forty years were required to write *Nihon Shoki*, and the production of *Shoku Nihongi* consumed 33 years. In the case of the former we may speculate that 40 years were needed to execute the difficult task of devising a fundamental structure for the history of Japan. The compilers had to adapt the form of the Chinese Standard Histories to the Japanese material, and then arrange the information in a satisfactory distribution. All this was done with a view to satisfying both the political purposes of the imperial state and the need for recognition of the regions and the great families. In the case of *Shoku Nihongi*, however, such creative and taxing intellectual endeavour was not necessary. The compilers only had to follow the format of *Nihon Shoki* and its Chinese models.

Yet this was not such a simple task, because they were pioneering in another way. *Nihon Shoki*, as we have seen, handled a variety of materials, such as legends and the contents of Chinese works. In contrast, the editors of *Shoku Nihongi* were the first to face the difficult task of basing a work exclusively on Japanese government documents. In 783 the first editorial team seems to have produced a draft that was unsatisfactory. The second team, headed by Fujiwara Tsugutada, shortened the manuscript from 20 volumes to 14, while expanding the coverage of the work. This suggests that the first team had not developed methods to master the documents and employ them judiciously for the narrative. As the historians became more skilful with each generation, the amount of time required to write a history decreased, as shown below. Another consideration is that those who worked on *Shoku Nihongi* had the most formidable task in terms of coverage. They had to deal with the reigns of nine Emperors, whereas the others dealt with one at the least and four at the most.

SIX NATIONAL HISTORIES

Title	Number of reigns	Number of volumes	Years in compilation
Nihon Shoki	40	30	39
Shoku Nihongi	9	40	33
Nihon Kōki	4	40	21
Shoku Nihon Kōki	1	20	14
Nihon Montoku Tennō Jitsuroku	1	10	8
Nihon Sandai Jitsuroku	3	50	8

The development of scholarly skill was probably a factor in progressively reducing the amount of time required to produce a history. However, we do not know how the skills were perfected and taught to succeeding generations. Unlike China, Japan had established no permanent office for the compilation of histories. At such an office the collection, preparation, and maintenance of records and documents could be handled as an ongoing task, aided by constant recruitment and training of scholars. Such an office would always have a variety of projects in various stages of completion: finding, classifying, storing, and retrieving materials; planning books and organizing scholarly teams; preparing drafts, integrating separate pieces, and consulting at high levels on matters of content and style, such as the use of characters in a manner not offensive to the Emperor. All this activity would create a body of scholars individually possessing diverse skills, and collectively capable of sophisticated work. In Japan, however, it appears that the scholars appointed for a history project established a new history office every time. It is not known how much continuity there was between successive projects. Since each history was separately commanded by the Emperor, we gain the impression that there was virtually no continuity among top level scholars.

However, there was a Fujiwara at the head of every one of the Five National History projects:

Shoku Nihongi	Fujiwara Tsugutada (727-796)
Nihon Kōki	Fujiwara Otsugu (773-843)
Shoku Nihon Kōki	Fujiwara Yoshifusa (804-872)
Nihon Montoku Tennō Jitsuroku	Fujiwara Mototsune (836-891)
Nihon Sandai Jitsuroku	Fujiwara Tokihira (871-909)

It is possible that this continuity of Fujiwara participation accounts partly for the uniformity of purpose and style seen in the Five National Histories: the family's own internal system of education may have provided for training in historical scholarship. However, this is only speculation, advanced in the absence of information about historical education in the period.

In summary, we see in the Five National Histories considerable progress in the development of skills. It took a long time to complete *Shoku Nihongi* because it was necessary to master the craft of selecting documentary materials and organizing them into a chronicle. The time required to compile the subsequent histories decreased steadily because the historians retained the form and improved their skills. We do not know how they were trained, but it seems likely that there was some continuity of personnel between successive works. This continuity may well have been provided by the Fujiwara family.

Imperial Bias

The most important aspect of the Five National Histories is that Fujiwara dominance on the editorial teams did not create a bias in that family's favour. Instead, the power and glory of the Fujiwara were separately displayed in another genre, called Historical Tales, which developed in the eleventh century. The character of the Five National Histories as chronicles of the imperial state did not change throughout the series. The procedure of methodical assembling of facts also remained the same. The writers of the Five National Histories worked entirely within the frame of reference of the imperial state presided over by the Emperors, and recorded all the historical facts they found pertinent. A century of this kind of writing clearly did much to reinforce the idea of the imperial state as the only possible form of government in Japan.

There was no effort to praise the good and blame the bad (beyond the conventional rhetoric applied to Emperors that was typically contained in decrees), and here practice deviated sharply from the Chinese models. In the Chinese histories moral causation was understood as the main force of historical development; it was necessary, for example, to view the founder of a dynasty as virtuous, and by the same token, the ruler who presided over its collapse was regarded as hopelessly bad. In *Nihon Shoki* this idea was transferred to the Japanese imperial line to account for a change in succession from one imperial lineage to another. Thus Emperor Nintoku, the head of a lineage, was shown as good, and Emperor Buretsu, at the end of the lineage, was shown as necessarily and completely evil. For the compilers of *Nihon Shoki* this presented no problems, since they seem to have known little about Emperor Nintoku, and nothing whatever about the awful Emperor Buretsu; thus no facts stood in the way of attributing total evil to him. They took the information for their narrative about both Emperors from Chinese sources.

The writers of the Five National Histories were also spared a contradiction between fact and value, not because they lacked information as in the case of *Nihon Shoki*, but because no major changes occurred in Japanese history in the period under study. There were no significant shifts in the imperial lineage, and no massive political disturbances. In this circumstance the entire frame of reference of the imperial state was taken as good without second thought, and the historians' only duty was to provide the record of facts. Thus in a strange way they were capable of detached historical scholarship.

Their main problem in selecting facts was not to take those that were politically acceptable, but simply to choose mechanically the most important ones out of an infinite supply. This choice had to be made in order to keep the work down to a manageable size. The material was entirely historical and not mythical, as was the case with *Kojiki* and *Nihon Shoki*. Therefore there was no need for the historians to intrude their own inventions into the materials or to rearrange them in any way. Nevertheless there were inevitably discrepancies and contradictions, and they took it as part of their task to correct them. These two purposes of selection and correction are clearly stated in the Preface to *Shoku Nihongi*: "By pruning what was redundant, we have retrieved what is essential and important; we have collected information to supplement what has been lost; we have adjusted the contradictions and corrected discrepancies in the overall narrative."[4] In the case of *Kojiki*, the imperial command to "discard the mistaken and establish the true" resulted in a work that is unreliable as history. The author was dealing with myths and had to create a framework to contain them. In the case of the Five National Histories, however, their complete subscription to the imperial system freed the authors from active bias. There was nothing that they were obliged to promote and nothing they were forced to conceal. Consequently there is nothing iniquitous about their purpose of "pruning," "adjusting," and "correcting." This is a practice of historians everywhere.

Modification of the Chinese Models

The strict annals form is modified in the Five National Histories, probably because the historians were trying to find the most effective means of narration. Satisfaction with the modified form permitted speedier production of the later works. The major change was to include biographies of persons at the date of their death, a practice that was started in *Shoku Nihongi* for persons of the third rank and above. It was broadened in *Nihon Kōki* to persons of the fourth rank and above, and in *Nihon Montoku Tennō Jitsuroku* to those of the fifth rank and above. In this manner the strict chronicle form was lightened by the biographical form, achieving in a different way the standard set by the Chinese classic, *Records of the Historian*. Sakamoto Tarō notes that the biographies in *Nihon Kōki* are unrelentingly critical, and those of *Shoku Nihon Kōki* are decorous, while those of *Nihon Montoku Tennō Jitsuroku* are warm and sympathetic.[5]

Along with the change from a strict chronicle form to a mixed form of chronicles and biographies, there is also a less praiseworthy trend towards limiting the scope of the histories while providing ever more details. That is, the period of time under study became shorter in the later works, but the details became more voluminous. *Nihon Shoki* was a major national history, but with *Shoku Nihon Kōki* and *Nihon Montoku Tennō Jitsuroku* the scope was reduced to the reign of a single Emperor.

Moreover, the historians began to feel unqualified to make a selection from the material available, feeling that it was presumptuous of them to judge unimportant some aspects of the august imperial reign. Every work carried a preface indicating the intentions of the authors, and they all noted that their work was pointed and selective. But when it came to the Emperors, *Shoku Nihon Kōki* put it plainly: "As for the activities of the Emperor, regardless of their importance, they are included without exception."[6]

Another deleterious development that took place in the Five National Histories was the noticeable tendency towards mechanical compilation of facts that were not highly pertinent to the history of the era. The last work, *Nihon Sandai Jitsuroku*, is filled with notices of good omens and natural calamities.

Perhaps this form of historical writing was beginning to exhaust its meaning and purpose. The Emperors under study in the last work, Emperor Seiwa (r. 858-876), Emperor Yōzei (r. 876-884), and Emperor Kōkō (r. 884-887) were not equal to the vigorous rulers and cultural leaders who had governed Japan when the series was launched. In fact, Emperor Yōzei was criminally insane and had to be quietly removed from the throne by the Fujiwara leaders. His successor, Emperor Kōkō, was chosen by them precisely in the hope that he would continue to display the ineffectiveness that made him a candidate for the position. Therefore the enthusiastic chronicling of all actions of the Emperor in the belief that they were all components of good government, may have begun to seem somewhat false.

The decline of the cultural leadership of the Emperors must have moderated the conviction that the act of writing history was also an act of good government. Thus the skewing of the later works towards voluminous recording of omens and disasters may be a symptom of malaise among the historians. No one intended to stop the historiographical enterprise of the state, but the court was incapable of producing another history after *Nihon Sandai Jitsuroku*. A work called *Shinkokushi* (New National History) was begun in the mid-tenth century, but probably was never completed.

In terms of political thought, it is clear that the Five National Histories powerfully reinforced the idea of the imperial system that was implanted into Japanese history by *Kojiki* and *Nihon Shoki*. It is impossible to measure the extent of reinforcement over the 100 years of their composition, but it certainly was great. Those who came afterwards could think in no other terms than the imperial system, even when it was in their own interest to do so.

PART II

ACCOMMODATING THE FUJIWARA REGENCY

CHAPTER 4

Historical Tales

The Fujiwara Regency

A new type of historical writing—Historical Tales—emerged during the long period of the Fujiwara Regency. The turning-point between the ancient imperial period and the classical era was the assumption by Fujiwara Yoshifusa (804-872) in 858 of the position of Regent (*Sesshō*). There had been other regencies in Japanese history; two aspects of Yoshifusa's regency made it distinctive.

First, the Fujiwara family were not members of the immediate imperial family. When the head of an aristocratic family took the position of Regent, it signalled the end of the line of vigorous Emperors. After Yoshifusa, the Fujiwara Regents solidified their control over the Emperors by making the position permanent and hereditary in their family. For generations they occupied the posts of Regents and Chancellor (*Kanpaku*) undisputed and unchallenged, and indeed the Regency lasted for more than a millennium, as a striking example of the persistence of political institutions in Japan after the loss of their function. The last Regent was Nijō Tadataka, a member of a recognized branch family of the Fujiwara, who was Chancellor from the 12th month of 1863 to the first month of 1867, and Regent from the first to the 12th month, 1867. Historians of the Heian period, such as the author of *Eiga Monogatari* (A Tale of Flowering Fortunes) and *Ōkagami* (The Great Mirror) inevitably saw the Fujiwara as possessing honour, power, and glory, and in their works they responded with enthusiasm to the success of the Fujiwara clan.

Notes to Chapter 4 are found on page 144.

Second, Fujiwara Yoshifusa was the grandfather of Emperor Seiwa. His rise to power was the result of assiduous and unswerving work at marriage politics by generations of the family, and this became the distinguishing feature of the period of the Fujiwara Regency. They worked to arrange marriages and inheritances to ensure that the incumbent upon the throne was under the power of strong Fujiwara family ties. Characteristically the position of Regent was held by the maternal uncle or grandfather of the Emperor. In addition the Fujiwara coldly sought to prevent the Emperor from attaining maturity and experience, and hence a sense of independence. Early abdication of Emperors became common after the tenth century, seldom by their own choice.

The Fujiwara Regency was also based on a changing administrative and economic system. The ancient imperial government consisted of a central government and a network of 66 provinces, ruled by Provincial Governors appointed in rotation by the capital. The rotation and discipline of Provincial Governors fell into decline, however, and in the tenth and eleventh centuries Provincial Governors tended to view the provinces as territories belonging to their own families. As a consequence, the flow of tax revenue from the provinces to the capital began to dry up. Landholding also ceased to function according to the design of the imperial state. Originally the state had assumed theoretical ownership of all land and tried to regulate it through a system of periodic reallocation. Its intention was to reallocate land holdings every six years, but this proved impossible. In 834 the reallocation period was changed to 12-year intervals; and then the entire reallocation scheme was abandoned in the early tenth century. In any case, it was never intended to apply to all the agricultural land of the country: aristocratic families and religious institutions were permitted to hold land exempt from reallocation. These holdings became the core of ever-expanding private estates (*shōen*), providing wealth and independence for the great aristocratic houses.

Everyone participated in the growing trend towards private estates, including the imperial house itself. In principle the imperial house remained tied to the imperial state based upon the landholding and taxation systems described in ancient law, but in practice it was obliged to join in the competition for private estates, in order to obtain income. Thus by the eleventh century, circumstances forced even the imperial family to work against the principles upon which the ancient imperial state had been founded.

The cumulative change over the centuries was great. These trends could not be described adequately by the style of historical writing found in the Six National Histories. The Six National Histories started as national histories, and *Nihon Shoki* is truly such, a work of considerable conceptual achievement, describing the origins and development of the nation and the state. As we have seen, the scope of the Six National Histories gradually narrowed, becoming primarily an account of the public acts of Emperors and government officials. Possibly one reason for the narrowing of the scope to the reign of a single Emperor was that the format had become inappropriate in changing conditions of society and economy.

New forms of writing were at hand, however, that were capable of describing some of the essential features of the period of the Fujiwara Regency. A genre known as Historical Tales came to be perfected by the eleventh century. It was a singular product of the Regency period. Historical Tales were extremely limited, being dedicated solely to describing the glories of aristocratic life in the completely secure society of the capital. But the new genre was able to direct attention to the centre of things, the Fujiwara family, without the sense of incongruity that would have prevailed if the National Histories had attempted the same. The National Histories were so closely tied to the doings of the Emperor that their meaning would have been diminished if the focus were shifted to a powerful family of the court.

The most important aspect of the Historical Tales was the fact that they did not challenge the concept of Japanese history as imperial history, which was established by *Kojiki* and *Nihon Shoki*. Historical Tales focused on the great families instead of the Emperors, but they showed no tendency to elevate the great families to a more important position. The authors literally could not imagine Japan without its Emperors.

Eiga Monogatari

Date and Author

The first history of the court in classical narrative prose, instead of Classical Chinese, is *Eiga Monogatari* (A Tale of Flowering Fortunes). The influence of classical narrative prose in literature is evident here, since most scholars believe it was written by a woman, Akazome Emon (fl. 976-1041) and it was women who were most important in devising the written form of Classical Japanese. All the Six National Histories had been written by men, and they used Classical Chinese. *Eiga Monogatari* is a work of 40 volumes, and it is widely held that the authorship of the first 30 volumes differs from that of the last 10. The work carries no preface to help with the dating, so it is not surprising that dating the work is a difficult problem of scholarship, inspiring many studies. The earliest possible date for the 40 volumes is 1092, the last year covered by the narrative; while the earliest possible date for the 30 volumes is 1028, the last year covered.

In the case of *Eiga Monogatari* and other such works, it does not trouble us to accept the 30-volume version vaguely as a work of the mid-eleventh century. Judging from the contents, it is certain that it was written fairly close to the events described, reflecting faithfully the conditions of contemporary life. In this respect it is unlike *Kojiki*, which was composed centuries after the events, when the author had very little idea of the circumstances of historical events.[1] The readers of *Eiga Monogatari* also shared the world of the history it describes, and this helped the work to succeed.

Akazome Emon is proposed as the author of the first 30 volumes of *Eiga Monogatari*, but this gives us little insight into the book. Instead, illumination works in the opposite direction. *Eiga Monogatari* would illuminate the poems of Akazome Emon, while her poems do not help greatly to interpret the huge quantity of material in *Eiga Monogatari*. Only external facts are known about her: marriage to Ōe Masafusa (1041-1111), widowhood, and subsequent entry into religion. Such facts are neither highly revelatory about the text, nor very different from the circumstances of other women of the period, so that little is gained by singling her out as the author.

Political Attitudes

As the first historical work of substance after the Six National Histories, *Eiga Monogatari* is important for its political attitude. The Six National Histories were chronicles centred around the Emperors with the specific aim of upholding the concept of the imperial state. Their success in making firm the concept is clearly demonstrated by the position of *Eiga Monogatari*, which accepted without reservation the succession of the Emperors as the framework for national life, even when its narrative was not mainly about the Emperors. The work places itself squarely in the sequence of histories of imperial Japan with its opening sentences:

> There have been more than sixty Emperors in this land since its beginnings, but I cannot describe all of their reigns in detail. I shall merely attempt to speak of the most recent.
> Once there was a sovereign called Uda....[2]

The narrative then passes through details of Fujiwara genealogy and proceeds swiftly to Emperor Murakami (r. 946-967), in order to praise him with conventional vocabulary.

The complex genealogies of the courtiers and especially of the Fujiwara were of great interest to the author of *Eiga Monogatari*. The only concept of historical explanation in the work is seen in the careful narration of genealogical ties; knowing the family connections clarified all matters for people of the period of the Fujiwara Regency. Thus, after the opening sentences regarding Emperor Uda and Emperor Daigo (r. 897-930), the narrative turns to the genealogy of the Fujiwara Regents, in detail that is tedious to modern readers:

Minister of State Mototsune, the Chancellor in those days, died during the reign of Emperor Uda. Mototsune was the third son of Middle Counsellor Nagara (Chancellor Fuyutsugu's eldest son, who was posthumously granted the title of Chancellor). After his death he was honoured with the posthumous name Shōsenkō. He had four sons, of whom the eldest, Tokihira, rose to the office of Minister of the Left and died at the age of thirty-nine; the second, Nakahira, became Minister of the Left and died at seventy-one; the third, Kanehira, held Third Rank; and the fourth, Minister of State Tadahira, served as Chancellor for many years.[3]

It is clear that absorption in these matters diverted thought away from the political nature of the imperial state and the propriety of the dominant position of the Fujiwara Regents.

Contents

The contents of the work are devoted primarily to the Fujiwara, and to the most powerful Regent of the period, Fujiwara Michinaga. He was probably the most skilful player of any era at marriage politics, and he arranged for the unprecedented ascendancy of the Fujiwara and of his own Northern branch (Kitake) in particular. At the same time he was a man of perception and vision, who transcended his narrow family interests in an effort to keep all the court families active and satisfied. This was accomplished by judicious use of his great power to influence appointments and to determine rewards and punishments. In addition he led the court to a grand scale of living, directing lavish entertainments and performances suitable to the capital of a great kingdom. Towards the end of his life he entered religion, but not before expressing satisfaction with his secular achievements in a poem:

> This world, I think
> Is indeed my world.
> Like the full moon I shine,
> Uncovered by any cloud.[4]

This man is completely idealized by the author of *Eiga Monogatari*. Fujiwara Michinaga dominates the work, and nothing derogatory or even critical is said about him. This is particularly evident in the last decade of his life, when he suffered from diabetes mellitus, together with cardiovascular complications. Diabetes in ancient times must have been a burdensome, debilitating, and embarrassing disease in severe cases, yet *Eiga Monogatari* does not note it. His real condition at the end, approaching death at the age of 62, was probably a diabetic coma. According to G. Cameron Hurst III, he was "a man desperately ill and nearing death, fighting a losing battle, and racked by persistent diarrhea, loss of control over his bowels, and painful boils."[5] In *Eiga Monogatari*, however, fantasy pervades the scene of the death bed:

> His only desire was to concentrate his thoughts on Amitabha Buddha as death approached. He wished to see no forms other than the signs and

attributes of the Buddha, to hear no sound other than the words of the Buddhist teachings, and to think of no object other than his future life. He lay facing west with his pillow to the north, his eyes on the signs and attributes of the Tathagata Amitabha, his ears filled with holy invocations of the Buddha's name, his heart fixed on the Land of Ultimate Bliss, and his hands grasping the braids held by the Amitabha statues. He looked the very image of a buddha or bodhisattva in human form.[6]

We know that the author had power to observe details and make critical remarks on small matters, and therefore the distorted image of Fujiwara Michinaga does not result from lack of ability. An example of the critical style of *Eiga Monogatari* is the astounding description of Fujiwara Michikane (961-995) as "an ugly, pasty-faced, hairy fellow, shrewd and domineering, with an ill-natured censorious manner that people found intimidating."[7] It appears that the importance of Fujiwara Michinaga was of such a scale that it overwhelmed these critical powers. Kawakita Noboru notes that *Eiga Monogatari* has an undeveloped appreciation of the world and of politics, and could not appreciate the complex unfolding of an event; the author simply had "poor analytical powers."[8] Yet in writing history it was necessary to deal with events at the high level of Fujiwara Michinaga, and consequently the author resorted to idealism and uniform praise of him. The deep cause of this inability of the author to penetrate the complex world of politics was beyond her control. Women of the court were completely isolated from government and business; their knowledge of worldly affairs came entirely from education and discussion, never from experience. The more profound understanding of politics in the next work, *Ōkagami*, seems to reflect male authorship.

Political Poetry

Eiga Monogatari excels elsewhere, in the recording of poetry. There are about 350 pieces, including Japanese Poems (*waka*), long poems (*chōka*), and religious verse, in the first 30 volumes of the work. By including such an abundance of poetry, *Eiga Monogatari* seems to record this aspect of history more capably than the Six National Histories.

One example of the use of poetry in *Eiga Monogatari* will indicate its importance in the text. Fujiwara Korechika (975-1010) became embroiled with Retired Emperor Kazan (r. 984-986), mistakenly taking the actions of the Retired Emperor as evidence of rivalry for the attention of Korechika's own lover. This was not unreasonable in light of the behaviour of the eccentric Kazan, son of the mad Emperor Reizei, and of his reputation for erratic actions in matters of the heart.[9] With his judgment affected by anger and jealousy, Korechika accepted the suggestion of his brother Takaie (979-1044) to intercept Kazan one night on his way home. The party fired arrows towards the Retired Emperor, with the intention not of killing him, but of frightening him. One arrow pierced his sleeve.

The government treated this affair as a major event, acting as if it had apprehended an insurrection. The capital city of Kyoto, especially the residence of Korechika, was placed under heavy security, causing tension among the populace. It was also revealed the Korechika had been practising privately a ritual known as Rituals in Honour of the Mystic King (*daigen*), which was properly celebrated only by the court itself, and this information was linked to an alleged plan of insurrection. Finally, a chronic illness of Empress Senshi was believed to be the result of curses invoked by Korechika. Eventually, after a period of anxious waiting, the brothers were banished to the western island of Kyushu, and they began their long journey into separate places of exile in the fourth month of 996. On the journey into exile Takaie wrote to his sister, Empress Teishi:

> At a place called Ōeyama, Takaie wrote an affecting letter to the Empress. "I have got this far without mishap. I am not good for much any more, but I feel certain that I shall return some day to be with you again, and my great concern is for your welfare in the meantime. I miss you dreadfully..."
> He added a melancholy poem:

> | Uki koto o | Ōeyama is, I know, |
> |---|---|
> | Ōe no yama to | A mountain of trials — |
> | Shiri nagara | Yet I had not thought |
> | Itodo fukaku mo | To encounter |
> | Iru waga mi kana. | Misery such as this. |

> "Such are my present emotions," he wrote.[10]

For the writer of the letter Takaie, as well as the recipient Teishi, and readers of *Eiga Monogatari*, it was the poem that carried the burden of the message. It is possible that by using the term *trials* (*uki koto*), Takaie made an association with a poem by Oshikochi Mitsune (fl. *c*. 900) in *Kokin Wakashū* (Collection of Ancients and Modern Poems, 905). He would expect Teishi to make the correct association and to recall the pain of Mitsune:

> Composed upon hearing the cry of the wild goose
> Mitsune

> | Uki koto o | My thoughts are filled |
> |---|---|
> | Omoitsuranete | With tribulations. |
> | Karigane no | The cry of the wild goose |
> | Naki koso watare | Comes to me |
> | Aki no yo na yo na | Night after autumn night.[11] |

The link with *Kokinshū* is made by the name Ōe no Yama, an ancient barrier station located on the border between the provinces of Yamashiro and Tanba. The name was popular among poets, being found

in six poems contained in five collections of the Heian period.[12] A pun on
Ōeyama and the verb *oboeru*, to remember, arises from the orthography
of the two words. Hence Takaie's poem

| Uki koto o | Ōeyama is, I know |
| Ōe no yama to | A mountain of trials |

suggests an association with the trials of Mitsune, thus asking Teishi to
recall his poem on suffering. Why Mitsune suffered is not known, but the
act of recalling his poem doubled the impact of Takaie's poem. All their
lives were in ruins, and *Eiga Monogatari* portrays this in the most
effective way with poetry.

Thus what began as an apparent attempt upon the life of the Retired
Emperor, linked to a political insurrection, resolved itself in the pages of
Eiga Monogatari into an exchange of personal poems.

Ōkagami

Structure

The personality and achievement of Fujiwara Michinaga must have been
very great, for he attracted the attention of a second historian in the
major work of the period, *Ōkagami*, which covers the period from 850 to
1025. The author is unknown and the date is uncertain, but it seems to be
of the late eleventh or early twelfth century. The title of the book is
interesting for its ambiguity, indicating the desire of the author to write a
great book or to reflect the greatness of its subjects, the Emperors and
aristocrats of the court. A less charitable rendering of "The Great
Mirror" is to understand it literally as a huge mirror, the biggest possible, made to reflect everything whatever. This might arise from a critical
view of the work as unselective of materials in terms of their importance,
and disorganized in their presentation. In any case the title influenced
later authors who also used the element of "mirror." These later works
are known as Mirror Pieces (*kagami-mono*).

Title	Date	Author
Mizukagami (The Water Mirror)	1185-98	Nakayama Tadachika (1131-95) or Minamoto Masayori
Imakagami (Mirror of the Present Day	1170	Unknown
Masukagami (The Clear Mirror)	mid 14th century	Attributed to Nijō Yoshimoto (1320-88)

The major achievement of *Ōkagami* was its successful adoption of the
annals-biographies form of historical writing originated by Sima Qian in

Records of the Historian. This form was an immediate improvement over the annals form because of the explanatory power inherent in its structure. It also had the capacity to provide more interesting discussion of historical characters, and some of the biographies in *Records of the Historian* were recognized as masterpieces of literature. In the same manner of biographies in *Ōkagami* are generally more informative and compelling than the sometimes stiff sketches given in the death-date entries in the annalistic Six National Histories.

In detail the structure of *Ōkagami* differs from that of *Records of the Historian*. *Ōkagami* follows the form as far as providing the basic annals of the Emperors and biographies of great men, but it omits entirely the chronological tables, treatises, and hereditary houses. Instead it provides a chapter entitled "Tales of the Fujiwara Family," and it concludes with "Tales of the Past." "Tales of the Fujiwara Family" may be regarded as an innovative adaptation of the annals-biographies form to the circumstances of Japan in the Regency period. This permitted the historian to take up aspects of the family, such as its inventory of shrines and temples, that were not easily placed into either the basic annals or the biographies.

"Tales of the Past" may reasonably be seen as a failure of the historian completely to adapt his material to the form. A chapter of such a nature is redundant in a work of history, which itself is an account of the past. In this chapter, anecdotes are introduced in a disconnected manner, and the significance of the matters narrated, which warranted their inclusion, is not immediately apparent. This leads to the previously mentioned interpretation of the title "The Great Mirror" as merely a mirror of huge dimensions so that as much as possible might be reflected. The standard for selection of materials was what the author found splendid or admirable (*imiji*), and unlike the compilers of the Six National Histories who severely pruned their materials according to strict criteria, he did not hesitate to put in everything he enjoyed: "Although I am afraid of appearing repetitious, I do want to mention all the things I have especially admired."[13]

However, it is not likely that readers of the Regency period experienced discomfort because of the overflow of material out of the structure of the work. Intellectual rigour was not a distinguishing characteristic of the period, as Heian aristocrats displayed a greater preference for literature and religion than for strict logic. In their daily lives they were occupied with questions of precise detail and observation of precedent in matters of ceremony, dress, and entertainments. Probably the extra material in "Tales of the Past" was savoured and appreciated for its contents, and there was no criticism of the work for failure of execution.

Even if we regard the last chapter as a failure of the historian, it does not significantly diminish the achievement of the work. The author of

Ōkagami purposefully organized the material of history into intelligible categories, thereby displaying intellectual command over history. His intellectual power is particularly striking in comparison to *Eiga Monogatari*, where the chapter themes arise from the materials themselves rather than the author's conception, and where the organization has no power to prevent the author from running on and on with more details.

Contents

Ōkagami is a national history of Japan, told in the form of a conversation between two old men who remember the events (old indeed: one of them, Yotsugi, is 190 years old, and the other, Shigeki, is 180). They meet by chance at a temple, and tell their entire story while waiting for the priest to appear. It starts with an entry on Emperor Montoku, the subject of one of the Five National Histories, and proceeds through the reigns of thirteen more Emperors, concluding in 1025, midway through the reign of Emperor Go Ichijō (r. 1016-36). Thus the author probably saw his work as a continuation of the national histories, despite the change in form from annals to annals-biographies, and the change in language from Classical Chinese to Classical Japanese narrative prose. However, if he kept the Emperors in mind, his heart was elsewhere, for the annals of the 14 Emperors are formal in nature, short, and uninteresting. Each annal contains the Emperor's genealogy, important dates (birth, investiture as Crown Prince, ascension, reign, and death), and tale of minor events and sometimes poems.

It was important for the development of political thought that the framework of the succession of Emperors was retained despite the lack of interest in the historical content of their reigns. As a work of considerable intellectual accomplishment and popularity, *Ōkagami* exercised great influence upon succeeding efforts, even beyond the Mirror Pieces. The author could have proceeded directly to the subject of Fujiwara splendour, since his actual interest was drawn more by the Fujiwara clan than by the Emperors. Conceivably this could have contributed to the intellectual foundations of a process whereby the Fujiwara clan made light of the Emperors, and developed into a line of kings of Japan. Instead, *Ōkagami* is explicit on the respective place of Emperor and minister of state: the Emperors are like the roots of a tree, and the Fujiwara are like the gorgeous fruit.

There are 20 biographies of Fujiwara men (and none of women) in *Ōkagami*, starting with a brief biography of Yoshifusa and ending with Michinaga. Of Yoshifusa's becoming the first Regent, *Ōkagami* merely says,

> He was a senior noble for about thirty years, a minister of state for twenty-five, and the first Fujiwara to act as Chancellor and Regent. We may well call him successful.[14]

Ōkagami refrains from further abstract discussion of the Regency and instead presents its explanation within the detailed narrative of the biographies. This method of avoiding theoretical discussion and working strictly with the substance of history is made explicit in the Preface:

> "I have only one thing of importance on my mind," he went on, "and that is to describe Lord Michinaga's unprecedented success.... It is a complicated subject, so I shall have to discuss a fair number of Emperors, Empresses, ministers of state, and senior nobles first. Then when I reach Michinaga, the most fortunate of all, you will understand just how everything came about."[15]

Mizukagami

After *Ōkagami*, the Mirror-pieces declined in both importance and literary interest.

Mizukagami (The Water Mirror) is thought to have been composed around 1185-98 by either Nakayama Tadachika or Minamoto Masayori; it follows *Ōkagami* in being written entirely in Classical Japanese, and adopting the format of narration by an aged person at a temple. However, it consists only of annals of Emperors, with 55 chapters devoted to the Emperors from Jinmu to Ninmyō (r. 833-850). It is not highly regarded because most of its materials were taken from *Fusō Ryakki*, a chronicle in *kanbun* of the Emperors from Jinmu to Horikawa (r. 1086-1107). However, *Mizukagami* is interesting in portraying some of the inventions of *Kojiki* and *Nihon Shoki* as indisputable fact; there was no motive for doing fresh research on these matters until the twentieth century. For example, when the invading ships of Empress Jingū arrived at Korea, the Korean king heard the sound of their war drums shaking the mountains, and thought, "There is a divine country to the east, called Japan. These ships must have been sent by that country. We had better not resist." *Mizukagami* also records as fact the benevolent acts of Emperor Nintoku and the wicked acts of Emperor Buretsu, but sees no particular political significance in them.[16]

Imakagami

Structure

Imakagami was composed around 1170 by an unknown author and was intended as a sequel to *Ōkagami*. The same conversation device is adopted, in which an incredibly old person is encountered at a temple and is coaxed into telling memories of times past. In *Imakagami* the author goes to Hasedera in Yamato Province and there encounters an aged nun. She is discovered to be a granddaughter of Yotsugi, the principal narrator of *Ōkagami*, and a few hours are spent until sundown listening to her tales. Although the conversation device is interesting, it is not maintained in the lively fashion of *Ōkagami*, where the remarks of

Yotsugi and Shigeki are interspersed throughout to give the impression of a lively dialogue, and to present their personalities and circumstances.

In *Imakagami* the narration is in the relatively lifeless form of a monologue. The personality of the old nun is not brought out past a tendency in the Afterword to Buddhist preachiness about the emptiness of words. This worry about writing books, when Buddhist doctrine condemned words as empty and indeed detrimental to the chance of rebirth in Paradise, was common among writers of classical literature. They always went ahead despite their anxiety, concluding that the harm might not be so great.

Although the nun does not come alive as in *Ōkagami*, the author takes advantage of the literary success of that work by reminding the reader of the connection between the two works. Chapter One, section "The Full Moon" (*Mochizuki*), begins, "When telling about the succession of Emperors, Yotsugi would discuss the Empress Dowager, so I too shall talk about the mother (Shōshi 988-1074) of this Emperor (Ichijō)."[17] Chapter Four, "Fujiwara," makes a similar reference:

> Yotsugi set out to describe the glory of Great Minister Michinaga, which he did in much detail. My purpose is to tell about his descendants. But if one does not know where the headstream is, one cannot understand the river current, so I must first speak briefly of Michinaga.[18]

No doubt the author hoped, by means of this association, to cause some of the appreciation given to *Ōkagami* to be transferred to *Imakagami*.

In structure the work resembles the annals-biographies form of *Ōkagami*. It displays the same loose fit between structure and materials:

1. Reigns of Emperors
2. The Fujiwara
3. The Genji descended from the line of Emperor Murakami
4. Children of the Emperors
5. Tales of the past
6. Things heard.

The chapter divisions provide only a rough guide to the materials which flow from one topic to the next. The book would be equally intelligible without them.

Bias Towards the Retired Emperors

The Six National Histories were straightforwardly devoted to the enhancement of the Emperors. *Eiga Monogatari* and *Ōkagami* unwittingly enhanced them further, even when their own attraction was towards the Fujiwara. Indeed, the author of *Ōkagami* could not make the material fit the structure because of his enthusiasm for the Fujiwara; he returned to the theme repeatedly in a disorganized way because of the great number of anecdotes that he wanted to supply. The same thing happened in *Imakagami*, but surprisingly, this time it is enthusiasm for the Emperors and Retired Emperors that dominates the work and spoils the organization. As demonstrated by Kanō Shigefumi, the persons of the Emperors figure in almost every chapter, whether as the subject of the basic annals, central figure of an anecdote, or background for an event at court.[19] This ruins the formal structure of the work, which would seem to confine accounts of the Emperors to the basic annals. Nevertheless, the interest of the author in the Emperors does not extend to political awareness. It is quite clear from the text that the theory of the state and the respective roles of the Emperor and over-mighty subjects hold no attraction for him. At most, it can be shown that he was a more or less unthinking supporter of the institutions of his own era.

The imperial house came to the fore of history once again, beginning with the reign of Emperor Go Sanjō (r. 1068-72). When he retired, Emperor Go Sanjō adopted a new line of independence from the dominant Fujiwara clan, involving a positive view of the long tradition of early abdication by the Emperors. The goal was to transform the position of Retired Emperor into one of power opposed to the Fujiwara, instead of a position of insignificance. There were no legal hindrances to their acquiring ownership of estates. Like the Fujiwara and everyone else, the Retired Emperors were free to try and acquire power and influence based upon private ownership of land, and in the eleventh and twelfth centuries they were quite successful. Lesser families than the Fujiwara seized the opportunity to associate themselves with the Retired Emperors and to offer services and funds to them. The legitimizing influence of the Retired Emperors for these people seems to have been no less than that of the reigning Emperors.

The diffuse nature of legitimacy in the ancient imperial state, extending beyond the reigning Emperor to one or more Retired Emperors, is virtually incomprehensible in terms of the modern concept of sovereignty. The problem could have been clarified by definition of the division of powers, but there is not a single document of discussion to that effect. However, it appears to have presented no difficulty to the people of that time, who did not trouble themselves to produce a precise analysis of the location of ultimate sovereignty. Thus the court of the Retired Emperor gradually became recognized as part of the governing structure of Japan from the twelfth century.

At first the jurisdiction of the Retired Emperors included no more than their own estates, but gradually their edicts came to apply in the public realm as well. This recognition of validity reached its highest point in 1221, when the command of Retired Emperor Go Toba was issued to destroy Hōjō Yoshitoki, who was deemed a traitor against the imperial state. This edict was sufficient to precipitate the Jōkyū War, which was the most important war in Japan after the Jinshin War of 672. However, no explicit political or constitutional theory developed to encompass this extraordinary rise to power of the Retired Emperors.

Therefore it must be said that *Imakagami* was not exceptional in its unreflective acceptance of the institution. Its historical evaluation of this institution is limited to a sentence of praise of Emperor Go Sanjō who began it: "Following the reign of this Emperor, the world was well-ordered, and the memory of him remains to the present day."[20] Otherwise it was simply taken for granted as part of the framework for the life of the court, which is the main subject of description. However, Kanō Shigefumi holds that the accounts of the Emperors of the period of the flourishing Retired Emperors are more vivid than the preceding ones, and he attributes this to the heightened interest of the author.[21]

Contents

It is noteworthy that the author wrote of tumultuous times, in which he himself lived, but did not record the major political and military events. With two major wars in 1156 and 1160, the seizure of power by the Heike, and their continuing use of force to settle political problems, the capital city of Kyoto was in an uproar for more than a decade preceding the writing of *Imakagami* in 1170. Yet the author took no notice of these events. His exclusive purpose was to describe the traditional activities of the court. The following passage, both vague and trivial, is typical of the contents of the work.

> There was an incident that sounded very elegant. In whose time was it, I wonder. It was the Empress of the middle period, probably either Shōshi the Jōtōmon'in or Teishi the Yōmeimon'in, during the reign of the Emperor of recent years. It was one of the rare occasions when the Empress came to the Inner Palace, and it happened to be a bright moonlit night. She said, "In olden times, on such a night the Inner Palace used to hold courtiers' receptions. How regrettable that there are no such events nowadays." The Emperor felt extremely ashamed. Just at that moment, moved by the beautiful night, there came a splendid voice singing the poem, "Ice sheets in piercing cold," and this sounded extraordinary. Then came independently a very resonant and reverent voice, reciting a part of the Sutra of the Doctrine of Immeasurable Volume, "First, the Buddha's tears fell." Each of them was a superb performance in its own way. The Empress said, "Even in olden times I never heard such performances. This is truly elegant." Because of this the Emperor's perspiration of shame dried, and his mind was relieved. So I heard. Was it the time of Retired Emperor Go Reizei, when Shōshi the Jōtōmon'in came to the Inner Palace? I wonder if it was true.[22]

Thus while the structure of *Imakagami* follows *Ōkagami*, it is closer in content and sentiment to *Eiga Monogatari*, which could not handle political affairs.

Imakagami can be criticized for providing a detailed history of the happier aspects of the life of the court and ignoring political reality. It is not even informative about the major events of the period, to say nothing of providing explanation. However, such was not the purpose of the author. Taga Munehaya regards it as useful in depicting the real life of the court. Based upon records, it is complementary to the *Tale of Genji*, which is realistic but imaginary.[23] The editor of the text published in 1957, Itabashi Rinkō, gives an even more positive appraisal:

> The essence of *Imakagami* must be sought in its history of art and literature. It does not go beyond the realm of gossip about art and literary circles; nevertheless it can be understood as an attempt at Japan's first cultural history.[24]

Conclusion

The complete absence of detached political analysis at the court during the Fujiwara Regency is appalling to modern thinkers. We wonder how they could ever have conducted their affairs without elementary classification of the powers of Emperors, Retired Emperors, Regents, and ministers of state. Perhaps an answer lies in the exceedingly slow pace of development. After all, 500 years elapsed between the establishment of the imperial state in 700 and its eclipse by the new military clans around 1200. In those 500 years all that happened was a shift of power from Emperors to Regents, followed by an attempt to re-establish imperial power in the hands of the Retired Emperors. Because of this slow pace, perhaps the distribution of powers was clear to everyone.

Yet it was of utmost importance that the changes were dealt with by historians. They retained the framework of the imperial state and the succession of Emperors—consciously in *Ōkagami* and without second thought in *Eiga Monogatari* and *Imakagami*—and fitted in the Fujiwara, who were the object of their admiring attention. There was no sense of challenge to the imperial state from this powerful family. Moreover they devised a literary form that was undoubtedly compelling for readers of the age, who had lost interest in the kind of annals found in the Five National Histories. Their interest was freshly captured by the conversation about the Fujiwara between Yotsugi and Shigeki in *Ōkagami*, and later authors used the conversation device to attract attention for their subject, notably in *Imakagami, Masukagami* (The Clear Mirror) and *Baishōron* (Discourse of the Plums and Pines).

Equally important, they made a precedent for handling the advent of new powers in the Japanese political system. The next group to arise, the warriors, contained much more potential for revolution than the Fujiwara, who were entirely the product of the court that they dominated. The warriors came from outside the court and possessed the power to destroy it. But the historians who discussed the warriors followed the example of the Historical Tales. They created a new form, War Tales (*gunki monogatari*), but that was the limit of their innovation. They too held unquestioning belief in the imperial system, and their writing showed the accommodation of the warriors to that system. This helped to form ideas that inhibited the behaviour of warriors at the moments when they held the power to destroy the imperial system: each time they refrained.

PART III

LEGITIMIZING THE WARRIORS

CHAPTER 5

The Rise of Military Government

Development of the Manor Economy

The political history of Japan consists of the repeated replacement of one ruling group by another within the structure of the imperial state. In the beginning there was symmetry of structure and power as the Emperors exercised authority according to the design of the system. We have seen that from the ninth to the twelfth centuries the Emperors were gradually displaced by the Fujiwara Regents. After the rise of the Fujiwara, another centre of power developed within the same structure, as the Retired Emperors of the late eleventh century began to compete for wealth and prestige. The tendency was always towards establishment of multiple power centres without renovating the formal state system or eliminating the earlier established powers. This is seen clearly in the Fujiwara rise to power in the Regency, an office that they simply added permanently to the governing structure. When the Retired Emperors attempted a political comeback, they too added another governing office without removing anything.

It is also remarkable that only the original work of founding the imperial system arose from programmatic thought. Seventh-century leaders such as Emperor Tenji and Nakatomi Kamako possessed a clear conception of the national needs of Japan, and they had a blueprint for state construction derived from Chinese history. The rise of the Fujiwara clan in the tenth century and of the Retired Emperors in the twelfth century came about as the result of conscious intention, but the goals of the builders consisted entirely of securing their own position and welfare

Notes to Chapter 5 are found on pages 144-45.

through pragmatic measures. The Fujiwara Regents of the tenth to twelfth centuries had no large-scale plans for building a new system of government; instead they were careful planners in their own self-interest and great opportunists. It is doubtful whether the Fujiwara Regents even possessed a concept of the state in the abstract, since we find no writings on the subject.

Thus there was a clear difference in attitude towards politics in the seventh century, when men planned and fought for the future of the Japanese state, and the Heian period when they schemed for position and wealth. This difference in political attitudes is reflected in the characteristic historical writing of the periods. The authors of the Six National Histories regarded their work as an essential activity related to building the imperial state and maintaining its rigour. The authors of the Mirror-pieces, on the other hand, had no sense that their work was an act of political leadership. They admired what had gone before, and they wrote of the past not to justify the rule of the Fujiwara clan (*Eiga Monogatari* and *Ōkagami*) or of the Retired Emperors (*Imakagami*), but to share with readers the pleasures of reminiscence. Despite the absence of ideology, however, their work reinforced the imperial system as the unquestioned framework for national life.

The pragmatic method was also followed by the next actors to enter the political stage, the military clans who came to ascendancy in the twelfth century. While they possessed a coherent view of their own way of life, they were completely without plans for constructing an appropriate state. Instead they followed the paths leading to honour and advantage as the Fujiwara leaders had done. The mainstream of their historical writing, War Tales, chronicled the times of the warriors and told of their glories in the same way that the Historical Tales extolled the glories of their subject, the Heian aristocracy.

The ultimate cause of the rise of the military clans was the alienation of public powers by the imperial state, the right to taxation and the right to secure public order. Both of these were progressively lost in the course of the development of manors (*shōen*), in a process sanctioned by the state itself. As early in the mid-ninth century, manors were being exempted entirely from taxation by means of an official document known as a charter (*kanshofu*). Since the trend towards manor development was universal, and since everyone sought this exemption from taxation, the necessary long-term result would be the disappearance of taxpayers. A stunning example was presented by Miyoshi Kiyoyuki (847-918) in his *Statement of Opinion* of 914, in which he drew attention to the case of Nima village in Shomotsumichi District in the Province of Bitchū. Citing the *Record of Climate* (*fudoki*) for the Province, now lost, Miyoshi claims that this district furnished 20,000 soldiers to Emperor Tenji, who was delighted, and gave the name Niman (20,000) to the village. This was later changed to Nima. But as a consequence of government neglect, the taxpaying population of the district declined precipitously. In the Tenpyō-Jingo era (765-767) there were only 1,900 registered taxpayers. During the governorship of Bitchū by Fujiwara Yasunori (825-895), registration stood at 70. When Miyoshi Kiyoyuki himself had governed, the registration had declined to nine persons. Finally, when Fujiwara Kintoshi returned to the capital in 911 from his tour of duty in Bitchū, Kiyoyuki asked him how many taxpayers remained, and Kintoshi replied, "There is not a single one."[1] Kiyoyuki did not proceed with the next logical question: What had Kintoshi governed? As a consequence of this decline, the tax revenue of the imperial government shrank, making it ineffective.

Law and Order

Manors were also granted freedom from entry by government officials. This meant that peace, order, and good government had to be provided locally, leading to the growth of families who made military prowess into a profession. The best-known names are those of the Genji and Heike clans. Another factor in the development of military clans was the early decay of the military and police forces of the imperial state. The absence of foreign enemies of Japan after the eighth century permitted the government completely to relax its military institutions. Facing only occasional eruptions of domestic rebellion, it allowed the conscript army provided by the imperial law codes to disintegrate, and relied on local recruitment to suppress provincial disorders. The imperial government was not even effective in policing the capital itself. The police institutions of the law codes were replaced by Capital Police (*Kebiishi*), instituted in 810, which in turn proved ineffective and corrupt.

Inevitably the citizens of Kyoto made private arrangements for their own protection, and as a result long-term relationships developed between the aristocratic houses of the capital and the military houses of the provinces. Clans such as the Genji and Heike supplied military protection to the aristocracy, and became known as their "teeth and claws." The Retired Emperors also established a private protective force.[2]

Domination of the Court by Military Clans

In the first half of the twelfth century there were many rivalries among opposing military clans, but no clash developed into a major war. Instead it was the aristocracy that precipitated the major struggles of the mid-twelfth century, when it called on rival bands to settle its own political disputes in the capital. These were the wars of Hōgen (1156) and Heiji (1160).

Sixty years later the historian Jien would note in his *Gukanshō* (Miscellany of Ignorant Views) that the Hōgen war marked the point at which Japan became "a warrior's world."[3] The Heike defeated the Genji, and remained in the capital to establish their own domination. Their regime was to last 20 years, and it marked the first stage in the political ascendancy of the warriors. However, they permitted Minamoto Yoritomo, the young leader of the Genji, to live, and he took advantage of an uprising against the Heike in 1180 to renew hostilities. For five years, from 1180 to 1185, Japan was plunged into the Genpei War which raged all over the country until the complete defeat of the Heike in 1185. It was the first war truly to excite the Japanese literary imagination, resulting in production of the masterpiece *Heike Monogatari* (Tale of the Heike). Early versions of this anonymous tale appeared soon after the event, and the tale became both a literary work and a performance in the hands of wandering blind priests with Biwa guitar, a peculiar form of history.

Founding of the Kamakura Bakufu

The administrative measures taken by Minamoto Yoritomo were more important than the battles. They led to the eventual development of a full warrior government, existing alongside the imperial government and possessing legitimate jurisdiction over warrior society.

Yoritomo gradually acquired enough power to make awards of land rights in manors (*shiki*) in reward for faithful and loyal service, and eventually he created *shiki* of a type that permitted extension of a new administrative system over Japan. This was known as the Steward (*jitō*), a position of financial management in the interest of the granter of the right. Yoritomo was the first to employ the *jitō shiki* for a public governmental system. Although his grants were made personally in the early stages of the Genpei War, a system of government was emerging by the war's end, so the stewards not only served Yoritomo personally but also acquired a public character and function. His right to make such appointments appears to have been formalized by the grant of his request in December 1185 to Retired Emperor Go Shirakawa to appoint *jitō* to "the manors of all the provinces."[4]

The complicated and compromised nature of the *jitō shiki* fully reflected the contemporary situation, in which a declining aristocracy and an ascendant military class became locked together as both antagonists and mutual supporters. Political initiative in the late twelfth and early thirteenth centuries lay entirely with Minamoto Yoritomo and his successors at the helm of the Kamakura Bakufu, and when their situation is viewed broadly, it seems that they could have accomplished the first political revolution in the history of Japan. Victory had been achieved over the major military rival, the Heike, and it remained only to establish secure rule over the rest of the military clans such as the Kajiwara, Hiki, and Wada. This was carried out in the first decade of the thirteenth century in a series of power struggles and short wars, as the Kamakura Bakufu leaders eliminated their rivals one by one. Then from such a great power base, the Kamakura Bakufu could have proceeded to seize the land of the aristocrats, displace them from office, and renovate or destroy the system of government.

The reason why none of this happened lay in the nature of the *jitō shiki* upon which the power of Minamoto Yoritomo and his successors rested. Normally the *jitō* was responsible for the affairs of the manor, especially its financial affairs, and for obtaining this right he was obligated to the Kamakura Bakufu. Yet in the great majority of cases the Bakufu did not own the manor. There was no need for such ownership, because individual Bakufu leaders and officials merely accumulated their own private property, like everyone else. There was very little need for public funds to sustain the government. Thus the manor to which a *jitō* was appointed continued as before under the ownership of aristocrats, temples, and shrines, who possessed income and management rights. The *jitō* was obliged to follow all established precedents, that is, to obey the law and serve his masters.

The interest of the Kamakura Bakufu was fully served by this arrangement, which provided both income for vassals and a means of control over the manors of the country. This control was what the imperial state lacked after it ceded the rights of immunity from taxation and entry by officials. In addition, the Bakufu protected itself against insubordination by over-mighty subjects by keeping them under the customary law of the manor and the command of the owners. Thus from the point of view of the Bakufu, a more satisfactory arrangement than the *jitō* system could not have been found.

In these circumstances a pervasive discontent existed in Kyoto, about which nothing could be done until a determined leader appeared. Perhaps to the general surprise, such a leader materialized in the person of Retired Emperor Go Toba, a gifted man.

The Revenge of Retired Emperor Go Toba

Clearly Retired Emperor Go Toba had great intelligence, and he was accomplished in arts as disparate as poetry and sword-making. In 1192 Minamoto Yoritomo had taken advantage of Go Toba's accession to the throne as a child to extract an imperial commission for himself as Great Barbarian-subduing General (*Sei-i Taishogun*), which was the position of supreme military command in Japan. Abbreviated to *Shogun*, this position was made the head of the Kamakura Bakufu and made hereditary in the Minamoto family until 1219. Retired Emperor Go Toba, however, objected in principle to the existence of the Kamakura Bakufu as an infringement upon imperial sovereignty, and he spent his life seeking ways to destroy it. As an adult ruler he would never have consented to bestowing the title of Shogun on Minamoto Yoritomo.

The Bakufu leaders were not intransigently opposed to the Kyoto establishment, and made friendly gestures towards it. Yoritomo travelled to Kyoto in 1190 and visited Retired Emperor Go Shirakawa, and in 1195 he came again for a service at Tōdaiji temple. The occasion seems to have been enjoyable, and he exchanged poems with his friend the Chief Abbot Jien, author of *Gukanshō*. Jien in turn was on intimate terms with Go Toba. Yoritomo's son Sanetomo (1192-1219) was even more strongly disposed towards the capital, and he actually became a friend of Go Toba, with whom he shared poetic interests and pleasurable (drunken) occasions. However, no amount of conciliatory behaviour by the warrior leaders could satisfy Go Toba, who continued in his unswerving aim of destroying the Kamakura Bakufu.

The other Kamakura leaders held the same opinion as Go Toba, that the apparently amicable relationship was false. Restive under a poet-commander who admired the Kyoto life too much, they solved the problem by means of assassination: Minamoto Sanetomo was killed at Tsurugaoka Hachiman Shrine in 1219, beheaded at a stroke by a swordsman who fled from the scene. With this link to the Kamakura Bakufu destroyed, Go Toba began to prepare actively for its overthrow.

The secret of Go Toba's preparations was not well kept, and the Kamakura Bakufu was ready in the fifth month of 1221 when he issued a decree naming the Regent for the Shogun, Hōjō Yoshitoki, a traitor and calling on loyal subjects to destroy him. Such was the beginning of the Jōkyū War, titled according to the year in which it occurred, Jōkyū 3. It is noteworthy that it was the imperial house, conscious of its tradition and unable to bear the humiliation of loss of sovereignty, that risked its own survival by declaring war. Otherwise the Bakufu leaders would never have fought against the imperial house. This helps to account for the absence of ideological statements by the Bakufu, or the warriors generally.

There was temporary hesitation in the councils of the Bakufu at Kamakura, but indecision was soon overcome, and armies were swiftly rallied to proceed to Kyoto. Unfortunately the imperial armies did not know what to do. Retired Emperor Go Toba was poorly served by incompetent advisers who recommended an unrealistic attack on the Bakufu, and then melted out of sight when the enemy appeared. It was all over in a month, with the Bakufu winning a complete victory and occupying Kyoto.

At that moment, the military leaders of the Kamakura Bakufu could have been poised for acts of revolution. They had fought directly against the sovereign of Japan and defeated him. The entire future of Japan lay in the hands of Hōjō Yoshitoki, his son Yasutoki (1183-1242), Minamoto Yoritomo's widow Masako, and a few senior advisers. But as noted in the discussion of the *jitō* system, they had no objection to the existing arrangements; in this they were unlike their sovereign and their vassals. Consequently their post-war settlement was based solely upon prudence and pragmatism. The situation required that Retired Emperor Go Toba and his advisers be disciplined, and this was accomplished by punishing them personally, without damage to their offices or the imperial system. Thus Go Toba was sent into exile on the remote island of Oki, where he ended his unhappy days in 1239. His sons, Retired Emperor Tsuchimikado (r. 1198-1210) and Retired Emperor Juntoku (r. 1210-20) were also exiled to separate places. The child Emperor Chūkyō, who had reigned only 70 days, was taken off the throne and replaced by the benign Emperor Go Horikawa (r. 1221-32). In an extremely conservative gesture, Go Toba's brother was placed in the position of retirement as Retired Emperor Go Takakura, although he had never occupied the throne of Japan. There was no regicide; execution was reserved for Go Toba's advisers, who were not, however, killed in great numbers.

These victors from the east were lenient. They also took the opportunity to acquire much property. As a consequence of the war, the power of the Kamakura Bakufu was greatly increased: it acquired clear domination over the court, established a permanent headquarters at Rokuhara in Kyoto, and acquired the means to extend its administration to the western provinces. None of this, however, had clear theoretical significance, and the Kamakura Bakufu leaders chose to make no remarks about the meaning of events. The task of interpretation was left to historians.

CHAPTER 6

War Tales

History, Imagination, and Literature

The rise of the warriors to dominance in Japan did provoke one interesting passage of direct political discussion. This occurred in the biography of a priest, *Myōe Shōnin Denki* (Biography of St. Myōe), which is discussed in the next chapter. What is more remarkable is the fact that such a major development as the rise of the warriors, the establishment of the Bakufu, and the defeat and humiliation of the imperial house produced such little discussion. Japanese thinkers did not want to confront the political events of their time by direct analysis. Instead, we find a continuation of political discussion by means of historical narrative. Just as the rise of the Fujiwara was reflected in the Historical Tales of the Heian period, the rise of the warriors in Japan was inevitably reflected in an appropriate historical literature.

War Tales, a new form of writing, performed two manifest functions and one hidden function. First, they recorded the lives and deeds of the warriors, as they carried out their missions, fought, and died. Simply to narrate what happened is the primary function of all historical writing. The second manifest function of War Tales was to create a warrior ethos and provide entertainment. They presented the essential values of warrior life by recounting tales of both the valorous and the faint-hearted, the victorious and the defeated, keeping alive the ideals, inspiring and encouraging each new generation to live up to the heroes of the past. The warrior way of life also provided entertainment with an abundant store of episodes. Perhaps only a small minority of the population was being

---

Notes to Chapter 6 are found on page 145.

educated in the ethos of the warriors, but nearly everyone could benefit from the entertainment provided by the War Tales. Life was drab for most Japanese of the twelfth and thirteenth centuries, a time of wars, plagues, economic crises, and famines, and War Tales transported them into a purer realm of high values and deep commitment.

This second manifest function of education and entertainment was probably more important in the long run than the plain function of historical recording. This was because the imagination of writers and raconteurs was captured by the tales of magnificent heroes and tragic losers. With their enthusiasm fired by the subject, the nameless writers and story-tellers were inspired to innovation, resulting in greater literary accomplishment. Thus the better literature is found in the works that glorify their subjects, such as the *Tale of the Heike*, while the less romantic works such as *Jōkyūki* (Chronicle of the Jōkyū War) are classed among the minor works of Japanese tradition despite their greater historical veracity.

In some cases, imagination soared very far, much beyond the invention of dialogue and the construction of details of place and appearance which were customary in all types of Japanese historical writing. For example, *Hōgen Monogatari* (Tale of the Hōgen War) is a conventional narrative of the events of the Hōgen War of 1156. It describes historical events in a mostly factual manner, embellished with descriptions and dialogue that may well be imaginary but not misleading. The work favours the young Minamoto Tametomo (1139-70), who was an uncle of Minamoto Yoritomo. It presents a romanticized view of his qualities and exploits, and thus far it is both a useful and interesting account. At the end of the work, however, Minamoto Tametomo is described as going to an Island of Ogres, inhabited by hairy people more than three metres tall, who spoke a strange language and said they were the descendants of ogres. At the point of Tametomo's appearance, however, they said, "Our good fortune has been exhausted, our treasures are lost, and our form has become that of men."[1] Tametomo took dominion over this island with no difficulty.

The case of Minamoto Yoshitsune (1159-89), younger brother of Minamoto Yoritomo, is even more striking. Yoshitsune is one of the most popular heroes of all Japanese history, a brilliant and courageous soldier who distinguished himself in the Genpei War. Yet he ended his days as a fugitive in north Japan, fleeing from the pursuit of his remorseless brother Yoritomo. He committed suicide at the last, having been betrayed by those to whom he turned for help. Numerous legends of strength, bravery, and wit adhered to the character of Yoshitsune, finding their way into all manner of theatrical performances. In the fifteenth-century work *Gikeiki* (Chronicle of Yoshitsune), these legends are abundant. Among the most enduring is his encounter with Benkei,

who was to become his valiant and faithful retainer. According to
Gikeiki, Benkei was anomalous at birth, having stayed in his mother's
womb for 18 months: he was the size of a child of two or three, covered
with hair and possessed of a full set of teeth. He grew to gigantic
proportions and, becoming a man, had his own way in everything. He
resolved to collect 1,000 swords by seizing them from people in the
streets of the capital. Having taken 999 and terrified the populace,
Benkei made the mistake one night of accosting Yoshitsune to take the
1,000th. Yoshitsune alone made him fight for the sword, and in the
combat Yoshitsune knocked away Benkei's sword, seized it, and leaped
to the top of a wall nine feet high. He threw the sword down to Benkei,
and then leaped down; as Benkei thrust at him, Yoshitsune stopped his
flight in mid-air, and reversed his direction to return to the top of the
wall.[2]

This kind of narrative is far from the historical recording of the Six
National Histories, as well as the more imaginative Historical Tales,
even after allowing for the peculiarities of those works. *Nihon Sandai
Jitsuroku* recorded as historical fact such things as the appearance of a
Grunting Ogre—a giant unworldly figure that appeared at the court and
gave horrible grunting sounds.[3] It also tells of the eating by an ogre of a
beautiful young maiden out for a walk with her friends.[4] Similarly,
Ōkagami included an account of a demon procession.[5] However, none
of these faithful recordings of the beliefs of the time resembles the
carefully crafted fictional account of Benkei and Yoshitsune, which
probably improved at every telling. This passed for history.

These are the manifest functions of War Tales—furnishing a record,
and providing education and entertainment. The hidden function was to
provide legitimation for warrior society and government. War Tales
were positive in outlook: they glorified and magnified their subjects, and
by literary means they moved their readers to empathy and to acceptance of the warrior presence. War Tales were not motivated by a quest
for political accommodation, yet they accomplished it. On the major
question of whether or how the imperial institution and the Bakufu might
divide powers, they had nothing whatever to say. On this point they
were even less articulate than the Historical Tales, which contained at
least an idea of the Emperor as the roots and trunk, and the Fujiwara as
the beautiful blossoms. Yet the War Tales were persuasive about their
general subject, and this enabled them to pass in silence over difficult
questions, such as those that had provoked Go Toba to action. Thus
Jōkyūki records Go Toba's edict that denounces Hōjō Yoshitoki as a
traitor; yet it offers no comment on the issues involved and merely
proceeds with the account of the war. For the author, the question was
already settled: imperial institution and Bakufu remained in place, and
there was nothing to say. This acceptance of the situation, which is
general in War Tales, amounted to a kind of legitimation.

The First Work—*Masakadoki* (Chronicle of Masakado)

There is considerable change in the form, style, and sophistication of the War Tales over the many years from their tenth-century origin to the last stage of theatrical performance in the Edo period. Let us examine some common aspects rather than attempt to discuss the entire development of the genre, which contains many more titles than the genre of Historical Tales; these are listed in Appendix C. We shall see in detail how the War Tales defused the great political issues by focusing on heroism instead of on issues.

The earliest work is *Masakadoki* (also read Shōmonki), which was written within months of the death of its hero Taira Masakado (d. 940). His rebellion, which occurred in eastern Japan at the same time as Fujiwara Sumitomo (d. 941) rose in west Japan, created a major crisis for the government. Masakado began with a private war in 930 against his own relatives in Hitachi province, and the scope of his activities gradually became enlarged, involving the imperial state. In 936 one of his enemies managed to have him declared a rebel by the government, but he was pardoned in a general amnesty in 937. His next escapade was a joint attack with Fujiwara Haruaki on government granaries, in what may have been a Robin Hood gesture to help the poor. This called forth an imperial army, which he defeated. Then in 939 Masakado began to extend a personal command over the eight eastern provinces, and finally in December of that year he had himself declared the new Emperor of the East by an oracle of the deity Hachiman. He then set about establishing a new imperial state that entirely resembled the old one. The oracle was simple and short, but powerful in its impact: "We give the imperial throne to the courtier Taira Masakado."[6] Imperial armies sent against him finally succeeded in the spring of 940, and Masakado died in battle in March of that year. His empire in the east vanished with him.

Masakadoki was composed in Classical Chinese, in a style that consists of alternating phrases of four and six characters. Some Japanese vocabulary and grammar are mixed in, but the adoption of Chinese imparts a briskness and directness to the narrative, which is further emphasized by its brevity. Like all succeeding War Tales, it takes the form of a simple narrative, starting with the beginning of a war and stopping with its conclusion. The rise and fall of Taira Masakado is told efficiently, and instead of enlarging at great length on the meaning of events, the author makes occasional brief reference to instructive incidents of Chinese history and to proverbs. The point of view is that of the ominscient recorder, and while the work clearly has sympathy for Masakado, the author is able to heighten the interest of the narrative by switching from Masakado to the court in Kyoto. This is particularly effective in describing the shock caused in Kyoto when Masakado titled himself the new Emperor and began making appointments to offices in a government constituted by himself. The worried Emperor Suzaku (r. 930-946) ordered prayers and services at temples and shrines to resolve the great emergency:

> I have had the honour to receive the Imperial throne; I have had the good fortune to continue the Imperial enterprise. However, Masakado makes disorder and evil into his strength and he desires to usurp the throne. Yesterday I heard of this; now he will surely want to attack Kyoto. I pray to the august gods that this wickedness be stopped at once; I look to the powers of the Buddha that this rebellion be dispelled immediately.[7]

Thus the major problem of Japanese history, namely the revolutionary potential of the emergent warriors, surfaced in the first work of War Tales. Declaring himself the new Emperor, Masakado made a direct and unprecedented assault on the imperial system. In addition to his distant claim through descent to the throne, Makasaso also seemed to claim the kind of legitimation that was most repugnant to the aristocracy: superior force. *Masakadoki* quotes a long letter that he wrote on the 25th day of the second month of 939 to the Regent Fujiwara Tadahira (880-949), in which he says, "In every history book one can see examples in ancient times [in China] of men who took the empire by wielding military power. What Heaven has granted to me is military skill. Consider, is there anyone to compare with me?"[8] Such a brutal view of power must have struck terror into the hearts of the aristocrats; it was the latent horror with which they lived through all the succeeding centuries of warrior development.

Significantly, however, Masakado did not follow up the implications of his own idea. In the letter to Fujiwara Tadahira, which is a deferential effort to explain his actions, he says that it was never his intention to begin a rebellion, but the actions of his enemies and the course of events led him into an uprising in one province. Since he was then a rebel, the crime was the same as taking 100 provinces, so he might as well proceed to extend his domain. This is by no means the rhetoric of revolution. Moreover, he makes apologies to Tadahira, whom he had served as a youth in Kyoto, saying "Although it appears that I am scheming to overthrow the country, how could I forget my former master?"[9]

In addition to Taira Masakado himself, the author of *Masakadoki* has no use for an idea of rule by force; on the contrary he condemns Masakado for his ambition: "Now, because of the rebellion of one man, disorder has arisen in eight provinces. Willfully indulging in such ambition is rare in both ancient and modern times [here the author is referring to Chinese history]. In Japan, right from the Age of the Gods, such a thing has never happened."[10] Thus the larger political implications of this warrior rebellion, namely the possibility of political revolution or of displacement of the imperial line from the throne, were denied in the first War Tale. This was important in setting the pattern for subsequent works, which in time came to provide a guide in real life for warriors. The movement towards warrior supremacy by displacing the Emperor was defused at the very beginning, by the actual historical failure of Taira Masakado to establish a new empire. In the work itself, Masakado's self-denying posture and the censure of the author eliminated any possibility of approving or encouraging revolution. Instead, other aspects of *Masakadoki* came to the fore in the succeeding tales, namely the portrayal of the valour, skill, determination, and prowess of the military hero. The celebration of struggle in battle, and the warrior way of life and death by self-disembowellment, became the main theme of the literature.

In other types of historical writing after *Masakadoki*, the implications of the rebellion were down-played in the same manner. *Ōkagami* assumes that the rebellions of Taira Masakado and Fujiwara Sumitomo, which occurred simultaneously in eastern and western Japan, were the result of collusion between the two men. It invents a simple dialogue between them, which bears no relation to historical facts: " 'I'm going to kill the Emperor,' Masakado announced. 'I'm going to be the Regent,' Sumitomo chimed in. And they pledged to work together so that one of them could run the government as he pleased while the other enjoyed an Emperor's life." [11] *Ōkagami* asks, "How could a scheme like that have succeeded in the face of the Court's authority?" This fanciful treatment of history, dismissing the possibility that the rebellion could succeed even in principle, shows how little the revolutionary potential of the rising warriors penetrated Japanese historical consciousness. Even *Jinnō Shōtōki* saw nothing of major importance in the rebellion of Taira Masakado. It displays a keen appreciation of the significance of warrior behaviour in Japanese society, and moreover defends the orthodox imperial system with a passion unrivalled in the history of Japan. However, the author does not seek out special causes in an attempt to account for any extraordinary aspects of the event, but simply refers to it as "a calamity of the times" (*toki no sainan*). [12]

Battle Histories

The aspect of War Tales as battle history rather than national history is much more evident in the second important work, *Mutsu Waki* (A Tale of Mutsu Province) and in all that followed. Composed perhaps in 1062, *Mutsu Waki* recounts the feats of the warriors in the Former Nine Years War which began in 1051 in northeastern Japan against the rebellious Abe clan. The terrain was difficult, the weather bad, and the foe formidable: perfect ingredients for the creation of a hero who would overcome everything. Minamoto Yoriyoshi (988-1075) leads his men to victory against such odds, and he is the focus of the work. The language is Classical Chinese, and hence the tale moves with a briskness and brevity similar to that of *Masakadoki*. At the end the author notes that he has used both official records and oral accounts, for he himself was not an eyewitness, but wrote as a historian in Kyoto. As a pure record of the subjugation of the Abe, the work is entirely devoid of political intent or ideology.

Subsequent works differ mainly in switching from Chinese to Japanese, thus becoming fuller and more expansive by including more detail. This expansion occurred because many of the works were produced, not by a historian in Kyoto sitting down with the documents, but by raconteurs who added details that they hoped would appeal to the audience. Thus the contents of the narratives changed with the passing of time. This was especially true of the works pertaining to the twelfth-century wars, *Hōgen Monogatari, Heiji Monogatari*, and *Heike Monogatari*, the last of which could be entirely recited.

This aspect of the tales account for their giving much attention, for example, to what everyone wore at the battle scene. The telling of the splendid appearance of the combatants, in the tense moments before the struggle began, heightens the expectancy of the listener. Similarly the recitative aspect accounts for the endless instances of warriors naming themselves before commencing battle. It is historically true that battle commenced with the adversaries calling out their pedigrees and challenging the best on the opposing side, but this made for such good recitation that raconteurs probably emphasized the feature. An example follows from *Hōgen Monogatari*:

> Among those rushing to be first . . . , a dweller in Sagami Province, Ooba Heita Kageyoshi, and his brother Saburō Kagechika moved into the lead and announced themselves: "When Hachiman Dono attacked Kanazawa Castle in Dewa in the Later Three Years War, Kamakura Gongorō Kagemasa, at the age of sixteen, charged in the van of the battle and while he had his left eye shot out and stuck to the first neck-place of his helmet by Toriumi Saburō, he took that enemy with his answering arrow. We are his descendants, Ooba Heita Kageyoshi and his brother, Saburō Kagechika."[13]

Oral recitation also explains the tendency to give long lists of the participants in battle. For example, for one of the battles in *Hōgen Monogatari*, the author gives 1,700 men as constituting the force led by Minamoto Yoshitomo, the father of Yoritomo. The text actually proceeds to name approximately one hundred of them.

In a text that was meant to be read, this would be ill-advised as inflicting deadly boredom upon the reader. However, we can assume that the enumeration of the 100 names was invariably enlivened by the techniques of recitation and by the skill and personality of the individual raconteur. Perhaps this recounting of names also had the purpose that we assumed in *Kojiki* and *Nihon Shoki*, which was to please those who appear in the list, or their descendants. In later works that were composed as written texts, however, the influence of this practice of naming combatants may have been unsalutory. For example, *Ōninki* (Chronicle of Ōnin), a history of the Ōnin War composed soon after its conclusion in 1477 by an unknown author, is almost unreadable because of its detailed site descriptions and lists of combatants. This has the effect of rendering virtually unmemorable the individual battles of a protracted war. It seems to counter the basic function of recording history events for the purpose of comprehension. Only a reader buoyed up by the hope of finding the names of his ancestors in the lists could make his way through the work.

Finally, the recitative aspect of the works renders innocuous any statements that tended towards political significance. In almost every work there are comments by the narrator about the will of Heaven with regard to how matters will turn out. Discussions among the characters are also common with regard to duty, the correct course of action, and the fate that awaits those who choose wrong. From the Hōgen War onward, the imperial house was frequently at the centre of the action, and therefore the declarations about Heaven bore upon fundamental issues of loyalty to the Emperor, and its opposite, rebellion. However, when presented in this context the declarations and discussions are not intended as serious examination of the political problem. They are eminently rhetorical, meant to lend more significance to the military action about to be described. Sonorous above all, they frequently ramble over so many aspects of political belief and theory that they illuminate nothing in the end.

This is not to say that War Tales have no philosophical point of view. They do, but it is a general philosophy of human life and not of action in the Japanese state. The prevalence of Buddhism is especially noteworthy. This philosophy is particularly striking in *Heike Monogatari*, which is a tale of the rise and prospering of the Heike, and of their downfall to utter ruin. The work is not one of celebration of war and warrior life, and certainly not one of cheerful praise for the victorious Genji, but of sorrow and sympathy for the once-great, once-proud Heike. It is tinged throughout with the Buddhist philosophy of the emptiness of glory and the inevitability of decline and decay; this is strikingly enunciated in the opening lines:

> The sound of the bell of Gionshōja echoes the impermanence of all things. The hue of the flowers of the teak tree declares that they who flourish must be brought low. Yea, the proud ones are but for a moment, like an evening dream in springtime. The mighty are destroyed at the last, they are but as dust before the wind.[14]

This gives the highest possible degree of significance to the events narrated, and in *Heike Monogatari* the War Tale is brought to its height. Yet we should hesitate to describe this as a high development of political thought in Japan. Instead, it is a virtuoso performance, linking literary skill together with received philosophy. Above all, *Heike Monogatari* is entertaining, and persuasive on the point of human fate, but we are none the wiser about political change and development.

Later Development

Like Historical Tales, which were devoted to the aristocracy, War Tales see only one thing, the warrior and his bravery and death. They are not national histories of Japan, and they can illuminate the life of only one social group. On the whole they do this very well. The history of the warriors comes truly alive in these works, primarily through their anecdotal narration. The focus of narration in all of them comes upon one individual after another, and they are allowed to come forward and make themselves known with their speech and actions. In this whirlwind succession of appearances the overall pattern of events is frequently lost to view; there remain instead images of individuals and their deeds of valour or treachery. Through the cumulation of acts and incidents a way of life also appears, that of the warriors and their families and followers.

In most fields of literature in Japan, the best works were produced quite early in the development of the genre. The *Tale of Genji* had few predecessors as a novel, and nothing that came after ever equalled its achievement. The *Pillow Book of Sei Shonagon* likewise was the best of its genre, with everything thereafter a pale shadow. This is true also of War Tales, which swiftly reached their height in *Heike Monogatari*. After it, the greatest literary achievements were *Taiheiki* (Chronicle of Grand Pacification) and *Gikeiki*; all the rest are minor. Among them are some that are much more reliable as historical sources, such as *Jōkyūki*, which narrates the Jōkyu War of 1221, and *Baishōron*, which records the rise of the Muromachi Bakufu under Ashikaga Takauji. These have received very little scholarly attention, doubtless because of their inferior quality as literature. Later works are neglected for possessing neither literary grace nor historical accuracy, such as *Shinchō Kōki* (Chronicle of Nobunaga) and *Nobunagaki* (Chronicle of Nobunaga), which relate the career of Oda Nobunaga (1534-82). However, the later works start to become interesting in a different way. They express the political philosophy of the early Edo period, when Buddhism was supplanted by Confucianism, and secular ways were sought to legitimize the new feudal domains that were founded upon conquest in the sixteenth century.

Taikōki (Chronicle of Hideyoshi) by Oze Hōan (1564-1640) is a record of Toyotomi Hideyoshi by the physician and scholar who served him. It abandons the medieval belief in reliance on gods and Buddhas, and centres on the hero in history, believing that his accomplishments arise from his own character and actions. In *Taikōki* there is also a belief that Heaven (largely undefined) always rewards the good and punishes the bad, and thus the development of history is not without larger significance. In this outlook, *Takōki* is a forerunner of the Confucian historical writing of the Edo period, which was based primarily on the Confucian philosophy of virtue rewarded by the approval of Heaven. However, as pointed out by Tamagake Hiroyuki, the later War Tale as seen in *Taikōki*, focusing on the accomplishment of an individual, was too simplistic to explain the origins and legitimacy of institutions. The War Tales could not satisfy the intellectuals of the Tokugawa period.[15]

With the coming of peace and the rise of the sophisticated historical and philosophical thought of the Edo period, War Tales died a natural death. They became drum-and-trumpet stories of no value beyond entertainment. They had no pertinence to warrior life, which the government of the early Edo period laboured to transform into a life of civil bureaucratism, and not engagement in battle.

PART IV

THE RIDDLE OF THE
DEFEATED EMPERORS

CHAPTER 7

Historiography of the Jōkyū War

The Shock of Defeat

The defeat of the imperial forces in the Jōkyū War of 1221 was shocking. None of the disasters that had befallen Emperors in previous times had the same immediacy, because they all took place within the court. After all, there was a long history of actual disrespect for the person of the Emperor, for example when Emperors were murdered or made to abdicate against their will by the Fujiwara Regents. However, forced abdication had been smoothly incorporated into Heian political practice without raising the question of its effect on sovereignty, or even of the sacrosanct nature of the Emperor's person. The exile of Retired Emperor Go Toba and the other Emperors by the victorious Kamakura Bakufu was therefore not unprecedented. What was shocking, however, was the outright confrontation between ruler and subject, in contrast to the stylized movement of politics in the old Heian court. The utter finality of the outcome was inescapable: the ruler had challenged his subjects and lost.

The Japanese imperial throne was fortified with theories that indicated that the ruler could not possibly lose. These were most clearly and succinctly discussed in the thirteenth century by the charismatic monk Nichiren (1222-82), who was a man of great intelligence, excellent perception, and forthright expression. Nichiren held his own views on most topics, and characteristically condemned the weakness of other views. With respect to the imperial throne, he seems to have thought that it could be saved by subscribing to his own doctrine of belief in the

Notes to Chapter 7 are found on pages 145-46.

absolute saving power of the Lotus Sutra. As discussed by Tamagake Hiroyuki, Nichiren presented the theory of the invincibility of the throne under three aspects of his various writings:

1. *Shinto*. The belief was universal that the imperial line had been founded by the Sun Goddess, who had vowed to protect it forever. Since the vow was eternal, the ignominy of defeat and exile was therefore incomprehensible.

2. *Buddhist*. It was necessarily true that the ruler was the most virtuous man possible. Only a person who had become qualified in previous lives and possessed 10 specific virtues could come to the throne. Losing the throne would be an impossible violation of metaphysical law.

3. *Confucian*. The ruler-subject relationship was absolute, and it was literally inconceivable that the Hōjō, lower in status than the Emperor, should have dared to oppose him.[1]

Thus the three major systems of thought in Japan all affirmed the invincibility of the imperial throne. Yet the intellectuals had to deal with the undeniable fact that the Emperors had been defeated. To solve this riddle was a formidable problem, which required innovation by the historians. Thus the outcome of the Jōkyū War caused Japanese historical thought to move forward, as seen in the works *Myōe Shōnin Denki* (Biography of St. Myoe), *Masukagami* (The Clear Mirror), and *Baishō-ron* (Discourse of the Plums and Pines).

Myōe Shōnin Denki

A rigorous examination of the problem is given in *Myōe Shōnin Denki*, a biography of the monk Myōe (1173-1232) of the Kegon sect of Buddhism. It is the most striking piece of political discussion in all of traditional Japanese thought. Myōe lived an independent life in the Togano-o hills near Kyoto, and by his strong dedication to the practice of Buddhist discipline he attracted eminent visitors, among whom was Hōjō Yasutoki, who had led the Bakufu forces against Kyoto. According to the anecdotal *Myōe Shōnin Denki*, they often held discussions and exchanged poems, and Hōjō Yasutoki sought the views of the monk on the deeper matters of life. During one of these conversations after the Jōkyū War, Myōe chastised Yasutoki for violating the imperial throne. The use of force, he says, might bring a temporary victory, but no firm rule can be established: "Since ancient times, there has been none who overpowered the country by force either in Japan or in China, and has been successful in maintaining his rule."[2] Myōe then goes on to lay down an argument of the absolute sovereignty of the Emperors, carrying the concept to its logical extreme:

> It has never been suggested that everything under the sun should not belong to the sovereign. It naturally follows, therefore, that you should not

be regretful on the basis of right or wrong when the emperor confiscates
your possessions. How could a man conceived in this land and conscious
of his obligations resist the command of the emperor, even if it forces him
to give up his life? If you would resist, you should leave Japan and go to
some other country, such as India or China.[3]

According to the account, Myōe's statement distressed Hōjō Yasutoki
to the point of tears, but he composed himself and countered with an
essentially Confucian argument. The measures at the time of the Jōkyū
settlement were taken for the good governance of Japan. It was the
misdeeds of the imperial government, including its unjustified attack on
the Kamakura Bakufu, that had caused the war. Nevertheless Yasutoki
was not satisfied with his Confucian response, and concedes the correct-
ness of Myōe's logical extremism in an astounding passage. He says that
he himself had already presented the argument to his father Hōjō
Yoshitoki:

> Are we to be punished for crimes we have not committed because of
> mistaken advice given to the emperor by the nobles? Still, everything on
> earth belongs to the emperor; fighting against him would be a violation of
> this principle. Therefore we should bow our heads, tie our hands, and go
> forward one by one to surrender and beg for mercy. And, after all, if we are
> beheaded, why should we regret it? Our lives are of no value when duty
> calls. We are powerless. But if we are fortunate enough to receive a
> generous pardon, we should spend the rest of our lives somewhere in a
> forest.[4]

This is just as hyperbolic as his description of the misrule of the imperial
government, but it is an important statement of the doctrine of absolute
sovereignty in Japan. We will find it repeated in *Masukagami* and
Baishōron.

However, the doctrine of absolute sovereignty of the Emperor is not
allowed to stand unchallenged. It is introduced in *Myōe Shōnin Denki* in
order to permit refutation by a superior argument presented by the
father, Hōjō Yoshitoki. Yoshitoki replies that the doctrine "holds true
only when the country is governed well," but in this case there was a
clear demarcation between the provinces under imperial rule, which
were in chaos, and the eastern provinces under the Kamakura Bakufu,
which were peaceful and prosperous. For the sake of the people of the
eastern provinces, it was necessary to resist the imperial attack.
Although Yoshitoki does not explain why the doctrine of good government overrules the doctrine of absolute imperial sovereignty (nor does
he cite any authority), it is clear that he regards his case as won. Perhaps
it was parental authority that made the case convincing when stated by
Yoshitoki, whereas Yasutoki had been overwhelmed by imperial authority and was ready to surrender.

Next, Hōjō Yoshitoki deals with the charge that they are violating the
imperial succession protected by the Sun Goddess. He has a clear
intention not to abolish the throne or even change the line of succession,

but merely to make the Emperor abdicate, and replace him with another prince of the imperial line. Here *Myōe Shōnin Denki* is realistic. In effect it points out that the deposition of Emperor Chūkyō and the banishment of the Retired Emperors after the Jōkyū War, which caused such great consternation, was actually not a violation of historical precedent or of the doctrine of the imperial succession.

This whole passage in *Myōe Shōnin Denki* is probably not a record of an actual conversation between Myōe and Hōjō Yasutoki. Rather, it is a striking piece of political discussion, all the more interesting for its rarity. The question of whether it is correct to resist the sovereign had arisen sharply upon occasion during the Heian period, and had not provoked political discussion. For instance, Emperor Yōzei was mad, and an entry in *Nihon Sandai Jitsuroku* suggests that he actually beat to death a courtier named Minamoto Masuru.[5] The entry notes that it was kept secret, but the murder is corroborated by Kujō Kanezane (1149-1207) in his diary *Gyokuyō* (Jewelled Leaves), which states in the entry for Shōan 2 (1172), eleventh month, twentieth day: "It is said that Emperor Yōzei was violent beyond compare. On one occasion prior to the Second Month Festival he drew a sword and murdered someone."[6] Emperor Yōzei was also a source of great trouble to the populace with such activities as his hunting parties, which rode heedlessly over the land destroying crops. Nezu Masashi writes that Emperor Yōzei was not insane, mainly because he lived to the age of 80, but that he was given to fits of frenzy.[7] Whatever his condition may have been, it became clear that Emperor Yōzei was a menace to everyone. Higo Kazuo et al. note carefully that "his behaviour was completely unsuitable for an Emperor."[8] However, no general case was ever made against Emperor Yōzei, who was quietly removed from the throne and taken care of by Fujiwara Mototsune (836-891). The incident passed entirely without comment, and there were no consequences for political theory.

Perhaps because of this tradition of pragmatic action, there was no direct response to the questions posed by *Myōe Shōnin Denki*. However, the questions were taken up again by the historians who wrote *Masukagami* and *Baishōron*. They showed awareness of the issues raised by *Myōe Shōnin Denki*, but they responded in the now-characteristic Japanese way, through historical narrative. In the process they softened the hard arguments about sovereignty presented by *Myōe Shōnin Denki*, and sought to persuade the readers to their side by means of convincing narrative presentation. *Masukagami* argued for the superiority of the Emperors, and *Baishōron* for the Ashikaga Bakufu, but neither of them discussed sovereignty directly.

Masukagami

Masukagami was the last of the Mirror-pieces, and the most intelligent. Its treatment of the Jōkyū War is actually only one aspect of its larger coverage of the question of court-Bakufu relations, extending from the time of Retired Emperor Go Toba to the reign of Emperor Go Daigo (r. 1318-39). Thus its perspective is informed by the knowledge of subsequent history, in which the Kamakura Bakufu fell in 1333 under attack by Emperor Go Daigo. That is, the events of 1221 were reversed a century later, as the imperial house was victorious, destroyed the Bakufu, and restored resplendent imperial rule. The author of *Masukagami* is thought to be the aristocrat Nijō Yoshimoto (1320-88), who is also famous for his literary activities. The work is presumed to have been composed in the period between 1333 and 1376, the date of the earliest manuscript.

Thus the author knew that Emperor Go Daigo won and restored direct imperial rule, but he also had the knowledge that this restoration was a total failure in the end. The restored imperial government proved to be incompetent, and loyal supporters faded away in a few years. Ashikaga Takauji withdrew from the restoration, and established a new Bakufu. Moreover, he also supported a rival line of the imperial house with the result that two imperial courts, the Southern Court and the Northern Court, existed in bitter struggle from 1336 to 1392. The author of *Masukagami* played a structural trick by deliberately ending the narrative in 1333, when Emperor Go Daigo returned to the capital in triumph to begin the new era, thus giving a glorified ending to the imperial saga begun by Retired Emperor Go Toba.

Tricks aside, in the second chapter *Masukagami* presents a succinct historical overview of the rise of the military clans, concentrating on the Heike and the Genji. Unlike the author of *Imakagami*, who could describe nothing but the imperial court, the author of *Masukagami* displays some command of the course of national history. He possessed materials for the history of the military clans as well as the aristocracy. Thus Minamoto Yoritomo's visit to Kyoto in 1190 is described, and his poems are recorded. The narrative becomes more detailed with the rise to power of Yoritomo, and it notes the important events in the rise of the Kamakura Bakufu such as the posting of *jitō*. In 1185 "Yoritomo received the title of Constable-General (*Sōtsuibushi*) and began to appoint his own men as Stewards (*jitō*). The decline of the nation of Japan began from this point."[9] Thus *Masukagami* is the first Japanese history to take account of institutional measures as significant in the course of national history.

On the other side, the hostility of Go Toba towards the Kamakura Bakufu is well demonstrated. The first chapter is devoted primarily to an account of his versatility as poet, anthologist, scholar, host of splendid parties, and excellent ruler. Also included is a famous poem expressing his lifelong hatred of the Bakufu, which is taken from the collection *Shin Kokin Wakashū* (New Collection of Ancient and Modern Poems, 1205). Given the topic "mountains" at a poetry contest, Go Toba composed:

Okuyama no	Making my way along it,
Odoro no shita o	Where it lies hidden under tangled thickets
Fumiwakete	Deep in the mountains,
Michi aru yo zo to	I will show the people
Hito ni shirasen	There is a path in this world.[10]

The path is that of the imperial government, and the thickets that obscure it are the Kamakura Bakufu. As the second chapter proceeds, the gathering storm of the Jōkyū War is depicted, and then the swift defeat of the imperial forces and the exile of Go Toba and the others.

Masukagami deals explicitly with the problem of the direct confrontation between the imperial court and the Kamakura Bakufu in two ways. First, the Bakufu leaders are shown to respect the Emperor completely, to the degree that they would have surrendered had the Emperor personally commanded his army. Hōjō Yasutoki says a moving farewell to his father Yoshitoki before heading for Kyoto, but rushes back the next day, full of doubt:

> But on the day following this unhappy parting, Yasutoki quite unexpectedly came riding back alone, applying the whip to his galloping horse. With heart pounding, his father asked, "What has happened?"
>
> "I understand our strategy and the general principles of battle as you have explained them," said Yasutoki. "But if along the way we should unexpectedly come upon a solemn imperial expedition flying battle banners and led augustly by His Majesty's own palanquin, what should be our strategy then? I galloped back alone to ask about this."
>
> Yoshitoki thought briefly before replying. "Well put, son! A good point indeed! It certainly would not do to take up your bow against the royal palanquin. Should you meet such an expedition, remove your helmet, sever your bowstring, and pay your earnest respects to His Majesty, placing yourself in his hands. If, however, His Majesty remains at the Capital while his troops are deployed against you, then fight heedless of life until your thousands are but one."
>
> Before his father had quite finished, Yasutoki was hurrying off again.[11]

Masukagami was following the same trend of argument as *Myōe Shōnin Denki*, but it stopped far short of the concept of absolute sovereignty of that work. Instead it introduces a single condition in which absolute sovereignty must prevail, namely personal leadership in battle by the Emperor. Needless to say, such a condition would never obtain, and everyone knew it. However, we should not conclude that it was merely an inane idea of the part of the author. Such an abstract formulation of the sovereignty of the Emperor, remote from any opportunity of realization, expressed a general sentiment that had never before been put into words. The concept of the Emperor was so awesome that the bravest and most accomplished warriors would bow before him. At the very least, the episode is arresting and thought-provoking, and would reinforce the ideas of the medieval reader regarding the character of the

imperial throne, however little it contributed to resolution of the conflict
between the throne and the Bakufu.

The second approach to the defeat of the Emperors is metaphysical.
Hōjō Yoshitoki as depicted as indecisive when the declaration of war
came from Kyoto. He wondered whether it was proper to resist, if the
Karma of previous existences had not brought these things to pass. But
he decided to fight, saying, "It is only a test of my own fate."[12] This
approach is resumed in the narrative of the postwar period, where the
author of *Masukagami* conducts a review of cases of battle against the
Emperor. The review indicates that defeat was impossible, and therefore its causes were mysterious and metaphysical.

> But among all these struggles, in this country there is virtually no other
> record of a subject of no status defeating an emperor.... Remembering
> these incidents [from Masakado to the Hōgen War], everyone thought it
> highly unlikely that this imperial court, consisting as it did of three ex-
> Emperors as well as the emperor could be destroyed. That it did occur—
> though it surely was not the result of affairs in this world alone—seemed
> all the more mysterious to the naive, confused people.[13]

Masukagami stops the discussion there, regarding the reference to
other-worldly causes as the end of the discussion rather than the beginning. A reference to extra-human mysterious principle reminded the
readers of the limits of investigation by the poor intellect of mortal men.
Since they believed in other worldly causation of all events, probably
their curiosity was satisfied by the explanation provided.

We have raised *Masukagami* for discussion in the context of relations
between the court and the Bakufu; this emphasis of the work is immediately apparent from the first chapter title. As in *Eiga Monogatari*, the
chapter titles are taken from significant passages within, and the first
chapter title of *Masukagami* is "Under the Tangled Thickets," from Go
Toba's anti-Bakufu political poem cited previously. The second chapter
is entitled "The New Island Governor," in reference to Go Toba's poem
upon his fate of exile to the island of Oki. His grand enterprise over, he
has become the ruler of a barren, isolated island, whereupon he calls for
sympathy from nature itself.

Ware koso wa	So it is I
Niijimamori yo	Who am the new island governor
Oki no umi no	Wild wind and waves
Araki nami kaze	Of the sea at Oki,
Kokoroshite fuke	Take care how you blow.[14]

Other chapters are titled more conventionally, with each title taken from
a less dramatic poem contained within. Although it is a political work in
its deepest intent, the bulk of it does not touch directly on the political
problems of the era. It is primarily a narrative of the life of the court,
written in a manner to compel the sympathy of the reader towards the

court. Its subject is the usual round of births and deaths, accessions and
abdications, court entertainments and artistic competitions. To make
the work more compelling for the reader, it is also filled with poetry. In
the analysis of Inoue Muneo,[15] there are about 50 poems pertaining to
the exchange of gifts, 60 pertaining to the rhythms of life of the aristocrats (that is, occasional pieces, not conscious literary creations), and
35 poems from times of disturbance, especially when Go Toba and Go
Daigo were sent into exile. Frequent references are also made to the *Tale
of Genji*, to remind the reader of the connection with the court in olden
times; Taya Raishun discusses 20 direct allusions to the *Tale of Genji*.[16]
Masukagami wins praise from modern scholars for its refined classical
style and its skill in selecting the best poems and tales from numerous
sources, of which the author had an excellent knowledge. Kidō Saizō
calls it the last great work of the aristocracy.[17]

The form of the work is a narrative by the now-familiar figure of an
aged nun who arrives at the Shōryōji Temple near Kyoto and is coaxed
into giving an account of the things she remembers. She discusses the
various works of history that bring the story up to the reign of Go Toba
and commences her tale there. It is clear that the author of *Masukagami*
intended his work to be a direct sequel to previous histories of the same
type. This is also indicated by the choice of *Masukagami* for the title,
which means "A Clear Mirror," but also has the meaning of "An
Additional Mirror."

In *Masukagami* the art of narrative was brought to the highest degree
possible within the form of Historical Tales. The author displayed excellent command of materials, intelligence in organization, and a skilful
classical style. The form itself, however, was limited in its capacity to
provide explanation of history. At best, Historical Tales could compel
sympathy for the subject that they favoured, and by all accounts
Masukagami is a superb piece of literature in depicting the court and
bringing the reader into communion with it. Yet the work remains
one-sided, incapable of sketching fully the national life of Japan, and
unable to explain why wars arose and why warriors eclipsed the court.
After introducing metaphysics to explain the major problems of history,
such as the defeat and exile of the Emperors, *Masukagami* stops. The
greater works of history, *Gukanshō*, *Jinnō Shōtōki*, and *Tokushi Yoron*,
would also introduce some such principle that regulates history. However, they go further, seeking to describe and explain exactly how the
principles apply. Thus they surpass *Masukagami* with their power to
explain the development of history.

Baishōron

The last work to take up the question of court-Bakufu relations in the
Jōkyū War is *Baishōron*. It is a pure War Tale, devoted to the rise of

Ashikaga Takauji to the head of a new Bakufu in 1338. The author is unknown, but judging from his detailed knowledge of the battles involving Ashikaga Takauji, and the absence of reliance on other sources, he was closely associated with Takauji's force. A possible date for the work is 1352, according to a passage that notes with regard to Emperor Go Daigo's exile to Oki in 1332, "More than twenty years have passed...."[18]

The title is derived partly from its adoption of the conversation device common in the Mirror-pieces, but not found elsewhere in War Tales. In this case the author goes late one night to Kitano Tenmangū Shrine in Kyoto, where many are gathered to meditate and pray. Kitano Tenmangū Shrine is noted for its plum trees and pine trees, and hence the title. An old Buddhist priest narrates the story of Ashikaga Takauji.

> The man who recorded this story did so at the Kitano Shrine, and so he wished for Takauji's glory to blossom forth like the plum trees and for his descendants to flourish for as long as the pines. He also had in mind the saying, "When the wind blows in the pines the plum blossoms send forth their fragrance." And so he called the book the *Baishōron*.[19]

Although the personality of the narrator is not brought out at all, the setting and the narrative device are ingeniously used to create a title of some significance.

As discussed by Tamagake Hiroyuki,[20] *Baishōron* does not view political questions in grandiose terms, seeking deep reasons for events. It narrates the matters at hand in a matter-of-fact way, and has a single pragmatic criterion for judging rulers, namely the quality of their governance. Provided that government is based on virtue, the country will be peaceful and the people will be prosperous, and the blessing of Heaven (*ten*) will be given upon ruler and people alike. This is a common concept of Chinese political philosophy, and its Chinese origin is evident in the frequent references made in *Baishōron* to precedents of Chinese history.

An example of the role of Heaven is seen in the fate of the Kamakura Bakufu in 1333. When the city of Kamakura was burned to the ground, it was attributed in *Baishōron* to the Bakufu's acting "contrary to Heaven's command."[21] In another example, the long struggle against the imperial forces was drawing to a close in 1336 and Ashikaga Takauji was in process of establishing his government, when the alarming news came that Emperor Go Daigo had once more escaped his guards. Everyone feared that he would become the centre of a new uprising and plunge Japan into yet more warfare. However, upon receiving the news Takauji was not unnerved. He explains that it was a great deal of trouble to guard the Emperor constantly, and that perhaps after escaping, His Majesty might be content to settle down quietly somewhere. "Fate," says Takauji, "is determined by Heaven's Way (*tendō*). It is not according to the power of the shallow intellect of man."[22]

The bias of *Baishōron* on the favour of Heaven needs little comment. It is clear that the author's observation of exceptionally virtuous government by Takauji, bringing forth the approval of Heaven, is not objective. Far from winning the spontaneous obedience of the people by virtuous government, Takauji spent almost his entire life in battle, attempting to establish his authority by the most primitive of rights, conquest. However misplaced, the idea of legitimacy through virtuous government is applied consistently throughout the work. The single exception is the discussion of the Jōkyū War.

The discussion between Hōjō Yasutoki and Hōjō Yoshitoki which we saw in *Myōe Shōnin Denki* is brought up once more in *Baishōron*, with Yasutoki raising the concept of absolute imperial sovereignty: "It has never been held that the entire land does not belong to the sovereign. Consequently, those who have resisted imperial orders, in both Japan and China, in ancient or modern times, have never been successful."[23] He feels regretful to be chastised because of the blow to the honour of his family, but "it is impossible to escape from Heaven's decree, so we should cease from battle and surrender."[24] Here Yasutoki is associating the will of Heaven with the concept of sovereignty rather than with the doctrine of good government. As in *Myōe Shōnin Denki*, Yoshitoki counters with the central principle of *Baishōron*, that the argument for surrender to the sovereign power is valid only if the sovereign's rule is virtuous. Yoshitoki elaborates upon the disorder in the provinces under imperial administration. In contrast, order and happiness prevail where the Bakufu is strong, and he concludes that "we should give battle and trust in Heaven."[25] Thus the central contention of the work is well established.

Then in the next passage Yoshitoki says, "If the Emperor resists, you must take off your helmet, lay down your bow, and surrender with your head bowed. This view also is not without some basis."[26] This is extraordinary because there is no indication in the entire work that the author has shifted the record of virtuous government onto the administration of Retired Emperor Go Toba. According to the political philosophy of *Baishōron*, only virtuous government would qualify him for absolute sovereignty. Therefore the argument for surrender because the Emperor is sovereign contradicts the argument of the whole work.

Persistence of the Imperial Framework

It is unlikely that readers of the medieval period were distressed by these breaches of logical consistency, any more than were Heian period readers. As much in the Kamakura period as in the Heian period, logic was overwhelmed by the force of belief. Although the organization of society changed greatly with the rise of the warrior clans, fundamental religious and political beliefs remained the same. In other words, the ideas that made the concept of the imperial state intelligible in ancient times remained in full force. For example, the most powerful support of the imperial house was the concept of the divine founding of Japan, as presented in *Kojiki* and *Nihon Shoki*. This belief was held without question by Minamoto Yoritomo, founder of the Kamakura Bakufu, who said in 1184, "Japan [literally, our Imperial Court (*wagachō*)] is a divine country."[27] Its universal nature is further demonstrated by the massive appeal to the gods of Japan, by both the court and the Bakufu, in the national emergency of the Mongol invasions of 1274 and 1281. Offering these prayers was a costly and time-consuming endeavour, undertaken with enthusiasm on all sides, and it called forth spontaneous individual expressions of national sentiment. A good example is the document bearing the prayer of the monk Ean (1225-77), which contains someone's fervent poem in tiny script in the margin:

Sue no yo no	At the very last days
Sue no sue made	At the end of the world
Waga kuni wa	Our country
Yorozu no kuni ni	Among all countries
Suguretaru kuni	Will still be the best.[28]

This concept of Japan's superiority was based squarely upon the nature of Japan as an imperial country. This means nothing less than a nation divinely founded and ruled by a succession of Emperors protected by gods forever.

These ideas about imperial Japan were shared by the historians. Our study of the historiography of the Jōkyū War has brought out the fact that they were obliged to use the imperial framework for their discussion. They were thoughtful men, yet they could conceive of nothing else. They were forced to work within the limits of this concept of the nature of Japan, and within the limits of the conventional forms of Historical Tales and War Tales. Thus they had necessarily to pose an insoluble problem for themselves: how could divinely protected Emperors suffer defeat and exile? As we have seen, *Masukagami* took refuge in religious doctrine, and *Baishōron* fell into a contradiction.

The failure of historians to give a satisfactory explanation arose from incorrect formulation of the fundamental rules for politics in Japan. The rule for legitimacy consisted only of ensuring that the succession of Emperors was continued. Under this rule, the actions of the Hōjō Regents in fighting against Retired Emperor Go Toba, and exiling the reigning Emperor Chūkyō and three Retired Emperors, were not illegitimate. *Myōe Shōnin Denki* said as much by having Hōjō Yoshitoki state that he would not abolish the throne or change the line of succession, but would only install a new Emperor. In the text, Hōjō Yoshitoki felt satisfied with that position.

The difficulty was caused by the introduction in *Myōe Shōnin Denki* of the doctrine of absolute imperial sovereignty, which was completely misleading as a concept by which to understand the facts of history. Under this formulation, *Masukagami* and *Baishōron* were unable to deal with the Jōkyū War. As a consequence they erroneously formulated the doctrine in terms of the personal invincibility of the Emperor if he were to lead his forces in battle. This was the only way out of the fourteenth-century impasse of thought. The theory of absolute sovereignty could be sustained in this way only because personal leadership in battle by the Emperors would never be a fact of history. No Emperor would ever be permitted to lead the way onto the field of battle, and therefore the doctrine of invincibility could never be contradicted by his defeat.

However, the task of historians is not to devise theories that are safe from contradiction because the events will never happen. Their job is to explain what did happen, by means of appropriate theories. Greater works of historical writing succeeded in introducing satisfactory theories, while retaining the basic imperial framework of history. The works of Historical Argument (*shiron*) to be considered next, surmounted the insoluble problem of the defeat of the Emperors by getting away from it, introducing instead general principles to understand the unfolding of human events. In doing so they elevated Japanese historical thought to the stage where it has universal appeal. The principles of the works of Historical Argument are meant to apply only to Japan, but in their essence they explain the general phenomenon of historical change in any society.

PART V

FROM IMPERIAL TO SECULAR HISTORY

CHAPTER 8

Historical Principles in *Gukanshō* (1219)

The Circumstances of Jien

Gukanshō (Miscellany of Ignorant Views) makes a great leap in Japanese thought. It is filled with anxiety for the political future of Japan, which seemed disastrous at the time of composition in 1219. In order to explain the impending disasters and perhaps to prevent them, the author introduced an original analysis of the past.

The anxiety for the future in *Gukanshō* arose from the circumstances of the author, who is generally recognized as the high priest Jien (1155-1225). Jien was the son of Fujiwara Tadamichi (1097-1164), who was Regent for a long period of 37 years (1121-58). Tadamichi was continuously engaged in struggles against his brother Yorinaga (1120-56), and their discord eventually became caught up in the larger problems of the imperial succession which finally resulted in the Hōgen War of 1156. The succession dispute and the ensuing war engulfed the bitter struggle between the father and the uncle of Jien, and eventually led to the collapse of the Heian political system and the rise of the military clans. Out of the turmoil of the wars of Hōgen and Heiji there arose the hated Heike domination of the capital, and then the national travail of the Genpei War from 1180 to 1185. The times remained unsettled because of the hostility of Retired Emperor Go Toba towards the Kamakura Bakufu. Jien's consciousness of this turmoil was acute: "From the time I was born, the world continued in complete disorder for seventeen years. When I was two years old, civil war [the Hōgen War] broke out in the seventh month; politics in China were also disordered;

Notes to Chapter 8 are found on page 146.

and ruler and subject alike were haunted by vengeful spirits." "My entire life has been spent thoughout in a world of disorder."[1]

In fact the disorder does not seem to have affected him personally, for he was well connected and had a brilliant ecclesiastical career. Upon the death of his father, Jien entered religion and rose rapidly to high rank, and eventually became Chief Abbot of the Tendai sect, the top position in the hierarchy of the Enryakuji Temple on Mount Hiei. Family and position brought him into the highest social circles, and he became especially intimate with Retired Emperor Go Toba when the latter was at the height of his powers. Jien's poetic abilities made him particularly attractive to the Retired Emperor. Thus he knew the mind of Go Toba well, and as he wrote *Gukanshō* in 1219 he had certain knowledge of the Retired Emperor's hope of destroying the Kamakura Bakufu.

On the other side, Jien also came to know the military leaders of the eastern provinces. As Japan's highest cleric, he had the duty of welcoming Minamoto Yoritomo when he came to Kyoto in 1195, and it appears that a genuine friendship developed between them. This close connection with the military leaders was to continue for the rest of Jien's life. As late as 1223 he received a gift of land in return for prayers he offered for the Shogun. This intimate association with both sides in the court-Bakufu dispute must have been a source of severe strain for Jien. A high priest of his stature would have been asked to offer prayers for both sides; but Jien, already an old man, luckily was sick for most of the period from 1213 to 1219. As he noted himself, "Fortunately I was ill at the time of the war, and escaped misfortune...."[2]

In addition to these public considerations, Jien had hopes for the success of his own Kujō branch of the Fujiwara family. His brother Kanezane found himself in a pleasing situation in 1219, when one great-grandson became Crown Prince, and another became the Kamakura Shogun Yoritsune (1218-56). It seemed then that court and military could be brought together, through the mediation of the Kujō family. Most scholars think that Jien's efforts to interpret history were influenced by a desire to show that historical forces were combining to produce this outcome of Kujō usefulness.

Purposes

Gukanshō was written, first, for the most simple and orthodox reason for writing history, to inform people about the past. Jien chose to write in the Japanese language rather than the abstruse Classical Chinese favoured for conveying difficult concepts, in order to make his work intelligible to all readers. He criticized the decline of scholarly standards in his own age, but regarding it as inevitable, he adapted his writing to the level of comprehension of the audience. Such was his own view; actually, among works of Classical Japanese, *Gukanshō* is now hard to read.

A second purpose of writing may have been to head off the impending war with a convincing admonition based on an understanding of history. It appears that he sent the work to Saionji Kintsune (1171-1244), a high-ranking aristocrat of the Kyoto imperial court who was also connected by marriage to the Bakufu, and thus in a situation similar to Jien.[3] He may have hoped that Saionji Kintsune might warn Retired Emperor Go Toba; but the plan did not succeed, and events took their course. This concern for the impending war accounts for the anxiety that pervades the work. *Gukanshō* finds that there are too many abuses and evil practices in the imperial government, and implies that such a bad government would be unwise to attempt a war against the Bakufu. There is an angry enumeration:

- ignoring the wise injunctions of Prince Shōtoku's 17-article Constitution, such as admonitions against envy and arrogance.
- swelling lists of appointments to superfluous offices ("If we look at the lists of appointments made at installation ceremonies, we will find no list with less than 40 new Captains of the Palace Gate Guards or Imperial Police").[4]
- the practice of bribery to obtain these appointments.
- excess numbers of Regents and ex-Regents, Abbots and ex-Abbots.
- decline in the quality of the Buddhist priesthood owing to the entry of idle and aimless sons of Regents and Imperial Princes.

In the arguments about virtuous government made by Hōjō Yoshitoki in *Myōe Shōnin Denki* and *Baishōron*, there was no evidence to support the contention that the imperial government was worse than the Kamakura Bakufu. But Jien, completely uninterested in the Confucian theory of good government, presents overwhelming evidence, thundering like a prophet. The state, he says, "has already been ruined, and we are now destined to have no men of ability."[5] Writing in this explicit manner, Jien hoped to awaken Retired Emperor Go Toba and his officials to their circumstances.

Jien also offered interpretive reasons for abandoning the anti-Bakufu movement. His interpretation of one of the Three Imperial Regalia (*sanshu no jinki*) was directly relevant to the question of military action. From time beyond memory the reigning Emperor possessed a sacred mirror, jewel, and sword, each of which originated in some mythical event. These regalia were given by the Sun Goddess to her grandson when he inaugurated the divine imperial rule, and thus they became symbols of imperial sovereignty.

In 1185 at the end of the Genpei war, the Heike fled from the capital with the child Emperor Antoku and the Imperial regalia of jewel and sword (the mirror was permanently kept at the Great Shrine of Ise). In the tragic sea battle of Dannoura Bay, described in *Heike Monogatari*, the Emperor's grandmother took the child Emperor in her arms, together with the jewel and sword, and leaped into the sea to drown. The jewel was recovered, but the sword was irretrievably lost. This was the significant point for Jien, who thought the loss of the sword must have meaning beyond a simple human accident. The incident became symbolic of the major development of Japanese history, in which the military functions of the imperial government gradually disappeared and were taken over by the military clans.

By this interpretation Jien tried to persuade Go Toba to accept the reality of historical development, of the inevitability and finality of the course of events. He hoped to make Go Toba and his court abandon their wild hope of destroying the Bakufu by making them realize that the political situation, however unfortunate and displeasing, had not arisen without good cause. This handling of the specific problem of court-Bakufu relations, by making an interpretation of a significant event, is typical of the approach found in *Gukanshō*. In this respect it is without precedent in Japanese historical writing.

In all other aspects of history, Jien conducted a similar search for causes. This thoughtful and extended consideration of the meaning of events makes it the first great work of philosophy of history in Japan. Unfortunately the accomplishment is not immediately apparent for modern readers, and for non-Japanese it is nearly unintelligible at first reading. This is partly because of the ambitious scope of the work and the profundity of its contents, and partly because of the organization, which is complicated and repetitious. It is also confusing, because the ideas presented and their relation to each other are not fully thought out. They are the reflections of a worried man who had no predecessors and no training in casting his mind over the whole of history, and who came late in his career to the task. Jien probably never expected to write *Gukanshō*: he was unprepared by his training, and perhaps even handicapped by a lifetime of ecclesiastical concerns. It is therefore appropriate not to criticize the work for its disorder, and to recognize instead its intellectual achievement in making an original interpretation of Japanese history.

Periodization

The structure of the work appears simple, but the argument is not. The first two chapters consist of a long chronology, compiled with the simple purpose of assisting the reader as he proceeds through the following chapters. The chronology begins with a list of the dynasties of China, and then continues with the reigns of the Japanese Emperors. The chronology of Japan begins with Emperor Jinmu, and is sketchy at the beginning. It lists all the important events of the more recent reigns, and it includes progressively more detailed lists of the chief ministers and high priests.

At the third chapter Jien begins his narrative and introduces the basic concepts of the book. The major idea, governing the structure of the entire work, is periodization of history. This is done according to cosmic factors entirely beyond human control.

Periodization is the simplest, most universal mode of explanation in history, so basic to understanding that it is scarcely noticed by most readers. It can be rooted in the fundamental concepts of a civilization, such as that of China which looked to a Golden Age, or in trivia. Even if it is only a shallow trick, giving a name to a period often provides immediate understanding. For example, the reader perceives that the people and events of a Golden Age have a special quality no longer attainable in subsequent eras. The incredible feats and long lives of the ancients become comprehensible if it is understood that they were performed in extraordinary times. In addition, the disorder and failures of later times or the present become intelligible by understanding that they occur in ordinary or especially benighted times. The artificial nature of the demarcation between periods generally escapes notice.

In Japanese historical consciousness there was a universal belief in the division between the Age of the Gods and the Age of Human Emperors, according to the structure of *Kojiki* and *Nihon Shoki*. But the existence of the Age of the Gods was merely accepted as simple historical fact, and writers did not attempt to discover the significance of the demarcation. Jien was the first to try to understand the significance of different periods of history.

The periodization of *Gukanshō* is based on Buddhist doctrine, that the history of the world is divided into three periods of the law:

1. Pure Law (*hōbō*), lasting 1,000 years after the death of Buddha
2. Imitation Law (*zōhō*), the next 1,000 years
3. Latter Law (*mappō*), the next 10,000 years.

As pointed out by Harada Ryūkichi, these terms are remarkably infrequent in the text. "Latter Law," and "Imitation Law" are used only once, and "True Law" does double duty as a worthy and correct principle as well as the name of a period. Nevertheless, there cannot be any doubt of the Buddhist nature of his periodization, based upon the common Buddhist thought of his times.[6]

Applying the schedule to Japanese history, Jien noted that the first year of the reign of Emperor Jinmu was the 290th after the death of Buddha, and that the date of entry into the period of the Latter Law was 1052. The outstanding characteristic of the period of the Latter Law is irreversible decline and deterioration of true religion and all human affairs. Knowing this, the reader immediately comprehends the necessity of unpleasant events and unhappy times. Thus Jien explains by simple periodization the decline of public affairs to the point of the currently impending catastrophe:

> The final years of the Ancient Age (*jōko*) and of (Japan's age of) True Law came in the final years of the Kampyō era (889-898). The reigns of Emperor Daigo (893-931) and Murakami (947-967) came at the tag end of that Ancient Age and at the beginning of the Medieval Age (*chūki*). Fine and noble things occurred then, but from the reigns of Reizei and Enyū (967-984) down through the Shirakawa and Toba (administrations as Retired Emperors from 1086-1156) the hearts and minds of the people only seemed to be the same. But since the close of the Go-Shirakawa reign (1155-58), there has been extreme deterioration; and the last 20 years (from the close of Go-Toba's reign in 1198) have been terrible.[7]

Clearly this periodization of history is not at all empirical; instead it was a straight application of current Buddhist doctrine. Belief in the Latter Law was widespread in Japan in the Heian period, and in Jien's time there arose popular religious sects based on the tenet. The Pure Land sect of Buddhism acknowledged the Latter Law doctrine, in which man is incapable of achieving enlightenment through his own effort and must rely on unconditional and absolute faith in Amida Buddha. As the first truly popular sect in Japanese history, Pure Land Buddhism rapidly grew into a major religion in the twelfth and thirteenth centuries, under the leadership of the monks Hōnen (1133-1222) and Shinran (1173-1262). Thus Jien's belief in the doctrine of the Latter Law and his extreme pessimism were both unexceptional and unoriginal.

Jien had a secondary periodization based on the concept of the Hundred Kings (*hyakuō*), which was borrowed from Chinese thought. As used in the *History of the Former Han*, in the biography of the philosopher Dong Zhongshu (179-104 B.C.), the term Hundred Kings means nothing more than "all the kings."[8] In Japan the term came to refer to the succession of Emperors, meaning "all the Emperors." It was believed that the deity Hachiman Bodhisattva had made a vow to protect the "Hundred Kings," that is, to guard the imperial succession forever. However, it seems that there was a change in this belief in the late Heian period, when the Latter Law thought began to flourish. The concept of the Hundred Kings came to mean that Japan was destined to have only 100 rulers, and no more. Jien shared this belief and mentions it at the beginning of the discussion: "I hear that after the beginning of the age of man and the enthronement of Emperor Jinmu, Japan is to have only one hundred reigns. Now that we are in the 84th reign not many more are left."[9] It is not clear what Jien anticipated at the conclusion of the 100th reign, but it is obvious that contemplation of the final days gave him a sense of urgency. He felt compelled to explain the principles that governed Japanese national life as it proceeded towards its inevitable conclusion.

Causation

Jien's most important work is his search for principles that govern history. Throughout the book he refers to *dōri*, meaning Reason or Principle, with regard to the events under discussion. The concluding seventh chapter is devoted entirely to a discussion of the laws of history.

It is necessary to distinguish his idea of Principle from logic, because his work displays no logical structure. The narrative chapters proceed in roughly chronological order, discussing Principle wherever it applies. The philosophical seventh chapter is not rigorously logical, but repetitious and confusing. Jien uses the word Principle 139 times, and in many different senses, as we shall see.[10] He makes no effort to rank his usages in order of importance, or to describe the limits of application of any use of the term, or to show how one kind of Principle is related to other kinds.

His system of thought has no architectonic qualities whatsoever, so every reader must strive to create a structure to contain Jien's ideas. Hence there are many possible interpretations. Nevertheless, Jien applied thoughtful analysis to the problems of history, and in every case he discovered something of importance. He found that events, difficult to comprehend in themselves, made sense when considered in the light of a particular Principle, or that Principle had acted as a causative force.

Jien was not alone in his use of the word. It is found in the legal documents of the Kamakura Bakufu as well, and its most striking use was in the vow sworn by members of the Council of State in 1232, to observe the principles of reason in their deliberations on matters at law. A solemn oath followed the 51 articles of *Goseibai Shikimoku* (Formulary for Judgments):

> In deciding upon matters of right and wrong, the members of the Council will disregard family ties and likes and dislikes, and will follow where reason (*dōri*) directs, stating their views according to the knowledge deep within their hearts, without fear of colleagues or powerful families.[11]

Kamakura Bakufu officials used Principle as both a procedural guide and a normative concept for law and policy. According to a tale in *Shasekishū* (Sand and Stones Collection, *c.* 1280), the Regent Hōjō Yasutoki was exceptionally devoted to Principle:

> He was truly a compassionate man, benevolent towards the people, and he appreciated the quality of reason (*dōri*). He was trustworthy and wise, and he had a reputation for mercy. It is said that he valued nothing more highly than reason (*dōri*), and responded with feeling, to the point of tears, to reason in the discourse of others.[12]

Thus the contemporary audience of *Gukanshō* was familiar with Jien's terms, if not the fresh and abstract way in which he applied them.

Writing before the Jōkyū War of 1221, Jien did not have to contend with the question of the defeat and exile of the Emperors. However, a good example of the application of his method is the case of the murder of Emperor Sushun. In all other historical writing there was a complete lack of interest in interpreting the assassination and judging its historical significance. *Nihon Shoki* merely records the event. *Gukanshō* is entirely different in asking outright, "Why was Emperor Sushun's assassination by Great Imperial Chieftain Soga no Umako in 592 treated as a great deed, warranting not the slightest punishment?"[13] First, Jien observes that killing Emperors is, after all, a crime. Therefore there must be a deeper reason for the event, a way of viewing it that transcends the apparent nature of the act as a crime.

Particularly difficult to interpret is the situation of the sage Prince Shōtoku, who not only failed to take action against the assassins, but actually came to power as a result of his family connection with the Soga clan. Jien proposes that the event was necessary in light of subsequent developments: Buddhism was firmly established in Japan by the Soga clan and Prince Shōtoku in the years following the assassination. This is according to the Principle that was in effect at the time:

> In reflecting about these developments, I find the essential point to be this: Imperial law (*ōbō*) was henceforth to be protected by Buddhist Law. These events occurred in order to manifest the Principle that, after the introduction of Buddhist Law to Japan, Imperial Law could no longer be preserved without the help of Buddhist Law.[14]

By this reasoning, everything is saved. It remains a crime to assassinate Emperors, but a particular Principle prevailed in this case, under which Buddhist Law was destined to be established. Prince Shōtoku knew this and adhered to the Principle of the situation, and thus his reputation as a sage does not suffer on account of his failure to punish the Soga clan for the murder of the Emperor; on the contrary, it is enhanced.

This is a remarkable piece of reasoning by Jien, which goes far to solve a difficult problem. The thrust of his argument is always to demonstrate the necessity of the events that took place, and not to condemn them. The same attitude prevailed in his effort to show that the Kamakura Bakufu had arisen for good reasons, and that it would be unwise for Go Toba to try and undo history. Of course, he fails to demonstrate the origin or existence of the Principle involved in the case of Emperor Sushun, or any case; he merely states it.

However, there was a collision of two types of Principle, one of Japanese law that it is a crime to kill an Emperor, and another, of Jien's own invention, that the Buddhist Law had necessarily to be established in Japan. This forced him to clarify the existence of a hierarchy of Principles: "And a second Principle was manifested [in the case of Emperor Sushun]: that some Principles are important and others less important and that an important Principle shall be embraced and a less important one rejected."[15] In this case Jien held that the Principle that the Buddhist Law must be established was the more important. But to prevent assassinations, the less important Principle would prevail in other cases.

This is not simply a matter of making an elaborate argument for a result favoured by the author—who was after all a Buddhist high priest and therefore well disposed toward the establishment of Buddhism in Japan. By asserting that there are many kinds of Principle, and that some Principles are more important than others, Jien uncovers the causative forces of history. As time passes and circumstances change, new Principles come into effect and supersede the existing Principle. What causes a new Principle to arise is not clear, but the fact that a new Principle has come into existence can be read in the events of history. We have noted a major case of a new Principle that the imperial government must yield its military function to the Kamakura Bakufu. This was symbolized by the loss of the sacred sword in the battle of Dannoura Bay.

The continuous advent of new types of Principle permits Jien to make a secondary periodization, within the framework of the three stages of the Law (True Law, Imitation Law, Latter Law). Jien isolates seven consecutive periods of Principle, beginning with the reign of Emperor Jinmu and continuing to his own day. His characterization of these periods is not distinguished by clarity, so we shall give only two samples out of the seven:

> 1. The beginning (of Japanese history) when the invisible was fused with the visible and when (visible) Principles were penetrated by (invisible) Principles. [Emperor Jinmu to Emperor Seimu (r. 131-190)]

> 5. The period of the Principle by which people would first divide up into two groups and contend bitterly against each other but then, because there was still one Principle (for this period of history), the group which was drawn to that Principle would win out and act accordingly. The Principle for this period was one that people did not originally understand, but it was one which required that when leaders with prestige and virtue (*itoku*) appeared in accordance with that Principle, those leaders would be used. [From the Hōgen War to the time of Minamoto Yoritomo.][16]

Arbitrary, vague, and unconvincing as this scheme now seems, this secondary periodization must nevertheless be recognized for its originality. It can be recognized as the first Japanese attempt to make a sustained application of a principle of historical understanding.

The periodic advent of new types of Principle does not exhaust Jien's ideas about causation in history. Less abstract and more conventional is the will of the gods. The will of the gods appears to work in conjunction with Principle, as in the rise of the Fujiwara clan to the position of Regency for the Emperors. The second major development of history, the rise of the military clans, is also seen as the will of the gods, and perfectly in accord with the Principle of the period:

I can not think that the destruction of all Taira descendants or the course of events for the descendants of Minamoto Yoritomo—who really pacified the empire and with an ability that was rare for either ancient or modern times—have been the doings of man. The ancestral Kami of the Imperial House (*sobyō*) have decided that soldiers are to control the state in this visible world (*ken*). This is now a requirement of, and in line with, Principle.[17]

It is a satisfactory outcome indeed for a philosopher when the causes he discovers work together in harmony. However, there was nothing Jien could do to integrate the acts of Heaven and of vengeful souls of both the living and the dead into his scheme of causation. They were left outside as random factors in history. Such were the appearance of comets, or strikes of lightning. In some cases the reason for the actions of the vengeful souls is known and the consequences limited, but vengeful souls could also act unpredictably, and the consequences of their actions are great, extending to the ruin of the state itself.

Jien's scheme for understanding history was not neat, but the allowance of random factors seems to render it chaotic. Nevertheless it was necessary to take account of ominous natural phenomena and vengeful souls, because their existence was universally believed without question. They were facts of life that could not be disregarded on the grounds that they did not fit logically into an explanation of history. Their acceptance by Jien probably caused him no logical discomfort, and certainly brought no criticism. All systems of thought contained the same element, and it was not regarded as distorting.

In addition to these odd factors in his thought, according to the research of Akamatsu Toshihide, dreams were important to Jien. A dream in 1203 about the imperial regalia took his attention for half a dozen years. His interpretations became extremely complicated, involving the Sun Goddess and the supreme Buddhist deity, Dainichi Nyorai, in relation to the position of the Emperor and Jien's own Kujō house.[18] Another dream of 1216 still occupied his thoughts as late as 1222 and 1224, when he referred to it in a written prayer. Akamatsu suggested that the 1216 dream helped motivate him to write *Gukanshō*.[19] Of course it was common for Japanese people of that era to guide their personal fate by their dreams, as it has been for most people at most times. But most of us forget dreams after a while. Jien's continuing interest in his dreams seem like an obsession.

Conclusion

Such are the major elements of Jien's philosophy of history. The Buddhist idea of periodization according to the Latter Law provided the fundamental divisions of Japanese history. Japan had entered into the period of the Latter Law in 1052, and this accounted for the main characteristics of national life. It was necessarily a period of decline. At a secondary level, the concept of the Hundred Kings provided a more precise timetable for the national decline of Japan. At the time of writing in 1219, the 84th Emperor Juntoku (r. 1210-21) was on the throne, and there remained only 16 more reigns until the end. What would transpire at the end is not clear.

Jien was original in moving beyond the conventional ideas about the age of the Latter Law and claiming that Principle was a fundamental cause in history. We have offered some criticisms of this idea, chiefly that Principle is an arbitrary concept, cast onto historical events, rather than an explanatory concept, derived from the study of the events themselves. In this respect, Jien's system shares the weakness of *Masukagami* and *Baishōron*. Their fundamental concept of the invincibility of the Emperors was also arbitrary, and was not derived from the facts of history. This made it difficult for them to give a convincing explanation for the defeat of the imperial house. However, Jien worked on a grander scale. His book is extraordinarily complex and yields numerous interpretations, because of the depth of the Buddhist concepts pertaining to the passage of time and the meaning of life cycles. We have not dealt with these. Our interest has been to show how the author came to terms with the changes that came over Japan with the emergence of the warriors, the establishment of the Kamakura Bakufu, and the loss of power by the imperial government. As we have seen, other works such as *Masukagami* and *Baishōron* found these processes incomprehensible according to their own ideas about the imperial institution. Jien found the processes unpleasant, and future prospects dismaying. However, he reacted creatively and sought fresh terms to make events intelligible. In the end, his system of understanding history in terms of the period of the Latter Law and the action of Principle imparted deep meaning to history.

CHAPTER 9

Historical Explanation in
Jinnō Shōtōki (1339)

The Imperial Schism of the Fourteenth Century

The Japanese imperial court of the medieval period had two debilitating shortcomings: recurrent bouts of competition for the succession, and fits of unfounded optimism about the possibility of destroying the military government. Together they almost caused the destruction of the imperial throne. In the turmoil surrounding the imperial throne in the thirteenth and fourteenth centuries, Kitabatake Chikafusa put forth great intellectual effort in his *Jinnō Shōtōki* (Record of the Legitimate Succession of the Divine Sovereigns, 1339). This work sought both to clarify the situation and to dispel the prevailing disorder.

The major cause of the succession problem was the absence of clear rules. The modern imperial succession is governed by fixed laws under both the Meiji Constitution of 1889 and the Constitution of Japan of 1947. In medieval times, however, the most important factor in determining succession seems to have been the wish of the most powerful Retired Emperor. This was guided as much by his personal feelings as by any concept of lineage. After the Jōkyū War it had become a tacit constitutional rule that the approval of the Kamakura Bakufu must also be given to the candidate arrived at by the contending factions in Kyoto; the Bakufu wanted to guard against the accession of another hostile Emperor like Go Toba. For most of the thirteenth century the Bakufu was relatively passive about the matter, paying no attention to any presumed rules of inheritance and seeking only to pacify the several

---

Notes to Chapter 9 are found on pages 146-47.

factions and generally keep the peace. However, the involvement of the Bakufu worked against it when the situation became over-complicated and it could not mollify all the contenders. The Bakufu then became the party to blame for dissatisfaction, and when it became drastically weakened in the early fourteenth century, it became the target for attack by everybody.

Briefly, there were two rival lines descended from Emperor Go Saga (r. 1242-46; Retired 1246-72). What the Kamakura Bakufu did was establish a principle of alternation between the two lines, and in the absence of final constitutional authority this became the only guide. Under this system of alternation, eight Emperors came to the throne, up to Emperor Go Daigo in 1318.

This alternation was a cause of unhappiness to everyone involved, and it also contained the seeds of a future schism. From the fact that both lines obtained the throne periodically, and that neither line was preferred according to some clear and established principle, it followed that both lines were equally legitimate. Only the power of the Kamakura Bakufu kept the situation under control, but it became increasingly incompetent in the late thirteenth and early fourteenth centuries.

It would have been in the interest of the imperial house as a whole to sustain the Kamakura Bakufu rather than destroy it, but of course they could not see this point. Once having destroyed it, they were unable to resolve their differences. The contending factions of the imperial house wound up in the worst possible circumstances: war against each other.

The second major weakness of the imperial institution was its misplaced optimism about eliminating military institutions. This optimism was found in abundance in Emperor Go Daigo. Resourceful and energetic, he was also mindful of the designs of Go Toba against the Kamakura Bakufu, and he became filled with resolve. Plot after plot ended in his exile to the island of Oki in 1332; this had been the place of exile of Go Toba, and the knowledge seemed to double the determination of Go Daigo. In the second month of 1333 he escaped from Oki and returned to Kyoto in triumph; Ashikaga Takauji, sent by the Bakufu to subdue the uprising, joined it instead, and finally in July 1333, Nitta Yoshisada (1301-38) led a force against Kamakura to defeat its armies and burn the city to the ground. The last Hōjō Regent, Takatoki, died by suicide at the Tōshōji Temple, together with some 500 followers.

The motivation of Go Daigo was a simple desire to destroy the Bakufu and to restore a government of direct imperial rule. According to *Taikheiki*, "it was hateful to his heart that the government of the court was set aside by the power of the military."[1] He regarded himself as the source of authority, and felt that a new world lay before him. According to *Baishōron*, he said "The precedents that are followed today were once the innovations of the past. The innovations made by me will serve in the future as precedents."[2] As pointed out by Satō Shin'ichi, innovations (*shingi*) were not well regarded in those times, and the word was used disparagingly, in speaking of "the lawlessness of present times," or "merchants nowadays." The emphasis in Go Daigo's statement, therefore, is on his own will as the source of innovations, and not on the importance of innovations as such. He was asserting imperial autocracy.[3]

Unfortunately for Go Daigo, imperial autocracy was completely illusory in a world of decentralized military power. Claiming jurisdiction over both aristocratic society and military society, he appointed aristocrats to many of the offices dealing with warriors. Their inexperience, ignorance, and hostility made the business of government into a muddle, and *Baishōron* describes the confusion that ensued, rather than the general peace and prosperity envisioned by Go Daigo:

> Meanwhile in Kyoto, where the Record Office and the Court of Settlements had been established, courtiers who were close to the Emperor nevertheless appealed to him directly, in extraordinary cases, about injustices. The Emperor's orders were issued in the morning and revised in the evening, so that people's fortunes rose and fell as quickly as the turn of a hand.[4]

By the time 1333 came to a close, "the warriors and courtiers were ranged against each other like fire and water."[5] It was only a matter of time until mass defections occurred and an open attack was launched against the imperial government. Once again Ashikaga Takauji changed his allegiance and attacked, and proceeded to set up his own Bakufu to take over the functions that the imperial government was bungling. Moreover, he presented as legitimate claimants to the throne pretenders from the Jimyōin line which was opposed to the Daikakuji line represented by Emperor Go Daigo. Thus a Northern Court (Jimyōin line) was established to rival Go Daigo's Southern Court (Daikakuji line).

The rivalry of the two imperial lines thus turned into a formal schism, and a war ensued between the courts that continued until 1392. Both sides suffered from the absence of the arbitration role played by the Kamakura Bakufu, which had held the dispute in check. The new Ashikaga Bakufu was not an arbiter, but a supporter of one court, the Northern Court. Its primary goal was to re-establish the accepted sovereignty over military society that had been exercised by the Kamakura Bakufu, and not to promote imperial sovereignty. This endeavour had only limited success, and Ashikaga Takauji spent the rest of his life in battle.

The war between the courts provided the formal alignment for many-sided struggles that continued throughout the fourteenth century and beyond, as armies ranged up and down Japan in seemingly interminable warfare. Numerous local wars also occurred in the fourteenth century that had nothing to do with the imperial schism, but whose participants formally declared themselves to be on opposing sides. The prestige of the imperial house was lowered by the schism, and perhaps it was saved from extinction only by this usefulness in providing legitimacy for the many private wars of the period.

The Circumstances of Kitabatake Chikafusa

In these circumstances of opportunism and disrespect for the Emperors, the unconditional loyalty of some supporters of the Southern Court is all the more remarkable. There can be no doubt of the genuine and absolute loyalty of Kitabatake Chikafusa. He was a court aristocrat descended from the line of the Genji clan which originated from Emperor Murakami, and was tutor to a son of Emperor Go Daigo. He remained on the margins of political life during the imperial restoration, but when Go Daigo fled from Kyoto to Yoshino in Nara Prefecture in 1337 to begin the long war, Kitabatake sprang into action. He directed the war effort for the Southern Court, maintaining the side against the greater force of the Ashikaga Bakufu by means of skilful organization and far-sighted planning. As we shall see, he understood very well the importance of the material life of man, and the connection that exists everywhere between loyalty and self-interest, but his own loyalty seems to have been pure and idealistic.

Like the other works of historical writing that we have discussed, Kitabatake's book was prompted by the political crisis involving the imperial house. For a period of three years from the autumn of 1338 to the autumn of 1341 he stayed at the fort of a supporter called Oda Haruhisa in Hitachi Province, directing the war effort from there. He was in close correspondence with allies and potential supporters, and perhaps it was natural in the period to write *Jinnō Shōtōki* also as a means of persuasion. He wrote under even more pressing circumstances than Jien. Living outside the capital, he had little access to books, and later wrote that he worked with only a single volume of genealogy.[6] Textual research has shown that this was not the case,[7] but he certainly worked under severely handicapped circumstances. He overcame this by his great learning, including knowledge of Chinese works, his powerful intelligence, and his unrivalled enthusiasm for the subject.

Assumptions

If *Gukanshō* can be called primarily a work of Buddhist historical thought, *Jinnō Shōtōki* is based on Shinto. It opens with a ringing declaration:

> Japan is the divine country. The heavenly ancestor it was who first laid its foundations, and the Sun Goddess left her descendants to reign over it

forever and ever. This is true only of our country, and nothing similar may be found in foreign lands. That is why it is called the divine country.[8]

There are several aspects to this beginning. First, from his reference to the eternal nature of Japan we see that Kitabatake differs fundamentally from Jien in his conception of historical time. In Jien's thought, time was measured, and a finite quantity remained in the current age of the current cycle. Jien thought there would be only 16 more imperial reigns of the 100 allotted to Japan by the principles of the universe. Kitabatake explicitly refutes such literalism, pointing out that "one hundred" can indicate limitlessness, as in the terms *hyakkan* (officials, literally the hundred officials) and *hyakushō* (farmers, literally the hundred families). The Sun Goddess vowed that the imperial line would continue forever, and nothing has changed to invalidate that vow.[9] Thus Kitabatake displays a fundamental optimism about the future because its duration is not governed by cosmic laws external to human purposes.

Second, the opening paragraph claims that the factors that govern the development of Japan are specific to Japan: "This is true only of our country, and nothing similar may be found in foreign lands." At first sight this may be taken as simple ethnocentrism, but in the context of Kitabatake's argument, it turns out to be a perceptive theory of cultural relativism. He considers the creation stories of India and China as well as Japan, noting where they are similar and where they differ. The important point he makes is the rational one that since India, China, and Japan are all in the same world, their beginning was necessarily the same; yet each country has developed a different theory about it: "Since all are of the same time and space, the beginning of the world was the same everywhere; yet each of the three countries has a different theory."[10] It is their respective theories, and not the absolute truth about origins, which must be honoured. Absolute truth about the origin of all countries is never under discussion. The values peculiar to Japan are therefore presented as valid on grounds of a general understanding of human society and history, and not on simple blind faith in what has been believed time out of mind. This rationalism is a striking characteristic of *Jinnō Shōtōki*. It is true that the work is based entirely on faith in the ancient myths of Japan, and it admits no other factors. Nevertheless it provides a rational framework for the myths. Observing that other countries such as India and China have their own myths, we accept those of Japan as natural and proper, and concede them as the basis for Kitabatake's historical argument. Thus his rationalism becomes the critical factor in persuading the reader to his argument, which is ultimately emotional.

Third, we turn to the contents of this opening paragraph. Japan is a divine land; it was founded by a heavenly ancestor, the Sun Goddess; the reign of the Emperors will be eternal. These were the staple ingredients of Japanese political belief, and the purpose of stating them was to invoke agreement with the historical argument that follows. No Japanese person believed anything else in those days, but as we have seen, political behaviour had not conformed to these premises. Hence Kitabatake restated them before proceeding to his guide for behaviour.

Causation

In his opening sentence Kitabatake succinctly laid out the assumptions of his work. The argument that follows is a demonstration of how the divine imperial succession has been carried on through changing historical circumstances. These include the familiar details of the rise of the Fujiwara Regency, the rise of the warriors and the establishment of the Kamakura Bakufu, the defeat and humiliation of the imperial house in the Jōkyū War. The new circumstances of schism in the imperial house must also be dealt with.

Surprisingly little attention is given to the specific case of the legitimacy of the Southern Court as opposed to the Northern Court. Kitabatake develops the general theory of divinely assisted imperial sovereignty, and elaborates upon the importance of the sacred regalia of office, but he pays little attention to the detailed history of their whereabouts. Perhaps this was because in his own mind the matter of legitimacy of the Southern Court was closed. At the end of the narrative of Emperor Go Daigo he writes,

> This is the fourth year since removal of the court to Yoshino in the province of Yamato with its ancient imperial associations. Inasmuch as the sacred mirror and jewels are at Yamato, how can it be regarded as other than the imperial capital?[11]

The regalia assume great importance in Kitabatake's thought as the symbols of office, verifying the true succession desired by the Sun Goddess, no matter what aberration appeared to have occurred by other standards. No more than anyone else, however, could he discover strict rules of succession. In addition, we have noted cases of assassinations and depositions, which suggest that the wrong person had somehow come to occupy the throne. Kitabatake could not account for all these in a satisfying manner, and the case of Emperor Buretsu stumped him completely. Emperor Buretsu died without any heir. The ministers of state elected as his successor Emperor Keitai, a fifth-generation descendant of Emperor Ōjin, of the line of his eighth son Prince Hayabusawake. Kitabatake says, "Perhaps the resurgence of Hayabusa's descendants was decided by Amaterasu herself, in which event its purpose cannot be comprehended by mortal minds."[12] Clearly Kitabatake resorted to faith to keep his theory intact. In view of the bewildering record of succession to the throne, it is difficult to see how he could have done otherwise.

The imperial regalia also seem to have possessed causative force in Kitabatake's understanding, but he does not rank it as the most important cause in history. He discussed the symbolism of the articles: namely, the uprightness (*shōjiki*) represented by the mirror, the compassion (*jihi*) represented by the jewel, and the determination (*ketsudan*) represented by the sword. These ideal virtues had real functions in the world of politics. If the uprightness of the mirror were applied, the Emperor would choose the appropriate men for office, and all would be well. If the compassion of the jewel were working, land would be apportioned fairly in accordance with correct principles. If the determination of the sword were at work, the good would be rewarded and the evil punished. If any of the three virtues were lacking, the consequence would be disorder.[13] However, there is no explanation of how exactly uprightness, compassion, and determination flow from the regalia into the political system. In his understanding, it was only necessary that the regalia exist, in order to guarantee the succession of Emperors and keep political life in good order by their respective special qualities.

After the power of the regalia, the second type of causation in *Jinnō Shōtōki* is what we may term secular historical explanation. All previous histories gave only a narrative of political and military events. As we have seen, this was generally insufficient to explain why events sometimes went counter to expectations based on morality and political theory. Kitabatake's work was the first in Japan to look behind events and recognize economic and social forces in historical development. This occurs not in his narrative history of Japan, as he goes through the Emperors reign by reign, but in the chapter on Go Daigo, where he pauses for reflection on the essentials of good government.

First he discusses the connection between land and political power from ancient times. Reviewing the system of merit lands under the Taihō system, he notes that good rulership lay in "preventing people from arrogating provincial and district lands to themselves and in checking the unwarranted establishment of tax-free status for lands." He cites medieval developments, in which manors were founded and, as a result of their immunity from official control, the country fell into chaos.[14] The effort of the state to recapture lands is noted, beginning with the reign of Emperor Go Sanjō, but,

> During the time of Shirakawa and Toba there was a great increase in new estates, and the range of authority of the provincial governors became a bare one-hundredth of what it had been. Thereafter the provincial governors did not even go out to take up their posts, but instead sent unqualified deputies to administer the provinces to which they had been assigned. How could the country have failed to become disordered?[15]

Previously, in the narrative of the reign of Go Toba, Kitabatake had discussed the importance of the institutions established by Minamoto Yoritomo:

Thus the Taira were destroyed, and it looked as though the emperor would truly rule over the country again as he had in the past. But Yoritomo's achievement was without parallel in history, and it was in fact he who came to exercise power as he saw fit. Moreover, since the emperor delegated authority totally to Yoritomo, the court's own influence declined even more. When Yoritomo assigned constables (*shugo*) to the various provinces, the authority of the provincial governors (*kokushi*) was thereby reduced and the office of governor became merely an empty designation. In addition, the appointment at this time of stewards (*jitō*) to all estates (*shōen*) and other private landholdings virtually rendered the office of estate proprietor (*honjo*) meaningless.[16]

Thus Kitabatake had a clear conception of the material and institutional basis of historical development. Although he repeatedly deplored the disorder that accompanied change, he managed to make intelligible the institutions and behaviour leading up to his own era. In this context, he returned to the critical question of merit awards in his own time and observed that the government of Go Daigo was unable to perform its expected function. In the discussion of Principle in the chapter on *Gukanshō*, we noted a deep-rooted, largely unquestioning belief by Bakufu leaders in the established institutions of society—family system, customary law, Bakufu offices and courts, Bakufu legislation. These institutions were built squarely on recognition of the relations between land and loyalty. Pure self-sacrificing behaviour was simply not expected. Kitabatake's understanding of institutions was similar. Commenting further on rewards, he wrote,

In general, the fact cannot be overlooked that when one person boasts of having received reward, there will be resentment among all the others. Suppose the Emperor, as sovereign of the country, were fairly to divide among all the people the finite amount of land available in Japan. If the method were to give one province to each, 66 people would take them all up. If the method were to give one district to each, Japan has 594 of them, so 594 people would be happy, and millions would be dissatisfied. Moreover, if they all took half of Japan, what territory would be left for the Emperor to rule? When such a grasping spirit arises, it begins to find expression, pervades everywhere, and becomes the origin of rebellion.[17]

More interesting than the fear of uprisings—Japan was full of them—is the assumption that acceptable principles for the workable distribution of land were not to be found in abstract thought. Abstract thought would always come up with something clear but impractical. Working principles were to be found in the actual institutions that had developed over time in response to changing needs.

In short, Kitabatake displayed the faith of the classical conservative that the historical distribution of wealth and power was valid, and in some sense a necessary result of the way things work. He did not condemn the system of power in the control of land, but rather recognized it as based on the principles acceptable under law and custom in his own time. This approach to understanding the development of institutions does not seem very impressive in the twentieth century, when it is the basis for every introductory text. In fourteenth-century Japan it was a considerable achievement to articulate the pragmatic assumptions of working society. It was all the more remarkable because Japanese political thought tended not to make explicit even such important matters as the constitutional distribution of powers.

On the basis of this understanding, Kitabatake was capable of intellectual acceptance of the rise of military power and the establishment of the Kamakura Bakufu, which infringed upon the power of the Emperors.

> If Yoritomo and Yoshitoki had not appeared during the disorder after the Hōgen and Heiji disturbances, what would have become of the people of Japan? Those who are ignorant of the nature of things will mistakenly believe that, for no reason whatsoever, imperial authority declined and the military were victorious.[18]

Recognizing the historical necessity of the rise of the Kamakura Bakufu, Kitabatake was not blind to the personal accomplishments of its leaders. He applied the Confucian doctrine of good government, particularly to Hōjō Yasutoki, and found that Yasutoki was upright and attentive to the needs of the people, even including the aristocracy. By maintaining his laws and following his example, his successors lasted for several generations.

Going beyond the level of personal virtue to the factor of the superior administration of the Bakufu, Kitabatake was at last able to solve the riddle of the defeated Emperors in the Jōkyū War:

> Since the age of Shirakawa and Toba, the ancient way of government had declined steadily, and in Goshirakawa's time armed rebellions occurred and treacherous subjects threw the country into disorder. The people of the land fell into almost total misery. Minamoto no Yoritomo restored order by his own force of arms; and although the imperial house was not returned to its former state, the fighting in the capital was quelled and the burden of the people was eased. High and low were once again at peace, and people everywhere submitted to Yoritomo's virtue. Apparently it was because of this submission that no one rebelled against the Bakufu, even at the time of Sanetomo's administration. How then could the Kyoto court expect so readily to overthrow the Bakufu, if it did not have an administration of merit equal to that of Kamakura?[19]

In *Myōe Shōnin Denki*, *Masukagaml*, and *Baishōron*, Hōjō Yoshitoki presented his government as the more virtuous, and therefore entitled to supremacy. The statement of superior virtue carried no conviction in those works. It is a simple invocation of a doctrine in support of one's own position; in those works Hōjō Yoshitoki can offer no explanation and no proof. Kitabatake's articulate discussion makes his case more convincing than any previous work.

However, what made his study important for nationalists of later times was not its sophistication in secular historical explanation but the third and most important type of causation that it recognized: the will of the Shinto gods. Kitabatake had utmost confidence in the power and desire of the gods to restore all things to good. Everything seemed to have gone wrong: rebellious subjects gave trouble to the Emperors; the Emperors themselves were sometimes unvirtuous; the succession to the throne was so tangled that Kitabatake could not reduce it to a system. Yet he asserted that the Shinto gods would save Japan no matter what the circumstances were:

> The way of Heaven and the will of the gods are always at work, so they will complete the fate of wicked humans by their destruction, and restore the world to its correct condition. This principle is true both in ancient and modern times. To know this is to possess a correct understanding of history.[20]

This is a pure statement of faith, hardly demonstrable by the facts of history, save to those who already believe it. It functions better as inspired and evangelical rhetoric than as a discovery of a law of causation in history.

In recognizing the superiority of the will of the Shinto gods, Kitabatake did not abandon regularity and predictability in human affairs. The gods are mysterious, but their actions are not random. They are guided by their goal of seeking the welfare of Japan, and indeed they are bound by the fundamental nature of Japan. In the same way the Emperors are bound by the fundamental nature of Japan; it is not only they who are divine. As Kitabatake put it in the most arresting sentence of the work, "All the people of Japan are divine creatures. Heaven will not permit the Emperor, revered as he may be, to seek his own pleasure while the people suffer."[21] This passage has no liberating intent. In modern Europe, the belief that each man is the child of God led to the assertion of individual rights, but nothing similar can be drawn from Kitabatake's statement. Instead, the divinity of the people marks the boundaries of evil: the gods will intervene to help when the people suffer.

Conclusion

Jinnō Shōtōki was popular with nationalists of modern times. First, it asserts the divinity and singularity of Japan. It also presents justification of the major political institution of the Emperor, together with a cogent explanation of historical vicissitudes. In 1941 the nationalist historian Tokutomi Sohō (1863-1957) received the weighty task of preparing a commentary on the imperial declaration of war against the United States and Great Britain, and he referred to *Jinnō Shōtōki* as a source for the ideology of imperial Japan:

> Chikafusa Kitabatake, the great patriot, statesman, scholar, and historian, pointed out to us in the first place that "Dai Nippon is a country of the gods." Why Nippon is a country of the gods is answered by the fact that it is a nation founded by the gods and also ruled by a deity.[22]

Tokutomi also quoted extensively from the discourse in *Jinnō Shōtōki* on the origin of the imperial regalia and their symbolism of the benevolent virtues of the imperial house.[23]

The position of Hiraizumi Kiyoshi was similar. He was a nationalist historian whose views dominated the History Department of Tokyo University in the 1930s. The period is still remembered with hatred by some of the scholars, such as Nagahara Keiji and Inoue Kiyoshi who were young history students during his regime.[24] Hiraizumi allowed his understanding of historical facts to be guided by his concept of *kokutai*, the national essence, instead of the other way around. In *Chūsei ni okeru Kokutai Kannen* (The Medieval Concept of the National Essence), a little book written in 1933, Hiraizumi observed a steady deterioration in thought from ancient times to the middle ages. The fourteenth century, of course, was the worst time, when the Ashikaga Shoguns seemed to have no concept of the national essence, because of their lack of imperial loyalism. But this situation called forth *Jinnō Shōtōki*, and Hiraizumi devoted the latter part of his book to an elucidation of its ideas. They are held to be a pure expression of the concept of the national essence which was current in Hiraizumi's time, the 1930s.[25]

Fervent nationalism, however, does not exhaust the meaning of *Jinnō Shōtōki*. Arai Hakuseki, the conservative rationalist scholar of the Edo period, had no interest in the gods or the divine nature of Japan, save as a curiosity of ancient thought that he had to explain. Yet Hakuseki appreciated *Jinnō Shōtōki* as a work of historical writing. In his own work *Tokushi Yoron* he quoted innumerable times from *Jinnō Shōtōki*, making it into his major source. His satisfaction with the work was based on its intellectual accomplishment in going beyond dogmatism and moralism. We have suggested that it advanced a secular explanation of historical development that did not violate Hakuseki's own Confucian rationalism.

Jinnō Shōtōki is the greatest work of historical argument of the middle ages in Japan. Possibly deeper meaning is found in the Buddhist philosophical concepts of *Gukanshō*. In addition, the Buddhist concepts dealing with the nature of time, and existence itself, have a universal character which is not shared by the Shinto ideas of the gods, which are peculiar to Japan. However, appreciation of these Buddhist concepts for history is dampened by the disorderly manner of presentation and argument adopted by the author, Jien. On the other hand, the ultimate causative force in *Jinnō Shōtōki*, the will of the Shinto gods, is a distressingly simple concept. Moreover, it is quite unintelligible without special instruction to anyone born outside Japan, for whom these gods with unpronounceable names cannot possibly exist. Yet the clear, forthright, vigorous manner of argument makes *Jinnō Shōtōki* the more compelling work. Writing in 1933, Kojima Yoshio confirmed the power of *Jinnō Shōtōki*:

> In order to write this article, I read *Jinnō Shōtōki* several times. The first time, I was not particularly moved. The second time, I felt that there were numerous small contradictions in the argument that are difficult to interpret. The third time, however, I realized that what seemed to be contradictions stemmed from a deep intent of construction. The fourth time, I was deeply moved by the passion and strength of *Jinnō Shōtōki*. If the primary purpose of writing a literary piece is to have power to win the heart of the reader, *Jinnō Shōtōki* achieves this purpose the best. If a work is to be considered great by achieving this purpose, then indeed *Jinnō Shōtōki* must be regarded as a great work of Japan.[26]

Yet passion does not persuade Western readers. More important, the work advanced the level of historical discussion in Japan towards rational, secular historical explanation. This type of explanation is based on discussion of the development of institutions, and their effects in both enabling and limiting the actions of people. Kitabatake Chikafusa himself was certainly not aware that the advancement of rational, secular explanation was among his accomplishments.

We have suggested that this was one of three ascending types of causation: (1) the mystical power of the three imperial regalia; (2) the role of institutions governing the behaviour of men; and (3) the will of the Shinto gods. In modern times, most historians recognize only the second type of causation, namely, the role of institutions. Although every person is entitled to a belief in the action of God in human history, the modern practising historian normally excludes this faith from his discussion. It is customary to concentrate exclusively on the circumstances of humans. That is why, in our estimation, *Jinnō Shōtōki* is greater than *Gukanshō*. The latter could not bring its philosophical concepts to bear on the points under discussion, except for applying the timetable for the expiration of the world. *Gukanshō* devotes its detailed narrative to the succession of Emperors and Regents, and mentions the institutions of *jitō* and *shugo* only once. Thus when *Gukanshō* notes a turning-point in history during the reigns of Emperor Shirakawa and Emperor Toba, when Japan became "a warrior's world," there is no deep secular comprehension.

In providing this secular explanation, Kitabatake Chikafusa made a breakthrough in Japanese intellectual history. Historical understanding was not confined to knowing the nature of the gods who lived nowhere else but in Japan. After Kitabatake, the history of Japan could become intelligible in terms and concepts that all the world would come to use—the terminology of secular historical explanation. It was for this reason that the modern rationalist Arai Hakuseki could make *Jinnō Shōtōki* into his major source without a trace of discomfort.

Considering the personal circumstances of Kitabatake, his achievement is all the more remarkable. He was passionately involved with the Southern Court, yet he was capable of detached historical understanding. People attached to the modern Japanese court in the nineteenth and twentieth centuries have been incapable of such detachment. This even extended to making judgments about the inevitable rise of the military clans at the expense of the imperial house. He was capable of recognizing virtue wherever it existed, even among the worst enemies of the imperial house, such as Hōjō Yasutoki. Fundamentally this was because he was not misled by his close association with the Emperors into overestimating the doctrine of the imperial state. He did not attribute absolute sovereignty to the Emperor. Kitabatake asserted that the sole important matter was the succession of Emperors as guaranteed by the Sun Goddess, and that was precisely the title of his book—Record of the Legitimate Succession of the Divine Sovereigns. If this were respected, every other historical development was intelligible and acceptable, whether it was the rise of the Fujiwara Regents or the development of the Kamakura Bakufu. Stating the imperial doctrine correctly, he was free from riddles about Emperors who were unvirtuous or were defeated in battle. Thus his great mind made its way onto the level of secular historical explanation.

CHAPTER 10

Secular, Pragmatic History in *Tokushi Yoron* (1712)

History After Kitabatake Chikafusa's Time

Gukanshō and *Jinnō Shōtōki* are called works of historical argument. A third study that is conventionally grouped with them is *Tokushi Yoron* (A Reading of History, 1712) by Arai Hakuseki. It brings to a conclusion the long line of discussion initiated by the construction of an imperial framework for history in *Kojiki* and *Nihon Shoki*, and continued by later works that attempted to solve the problem of contradiction of imperial values by the actual events of history: everyone believed in the Emperors, but many mistreated them. In addition, the ideology of the imperial house did nothing to save it from resistance against itself and from defeat in war. It is noteworthy that the tradition of historical writing in Japan retained a dogged adherence to realism in dealing with this contradiction between values and facts. We have seen that some types of historical writing gave a certain play to imagination, as in Historical Tales, which idealized the Fujiwara clan, and the War Tales, which romanticized the life of the warriors. But these were precisely the works that did not attempt to deal with the question of the indignities and insults given to the Emperors. The Historical Tales and War Tales, as we have noted, were one-sided, devoted only to describing the glories of the aristocracy and the warriors respectively. However, the works that retained a national focus and dealt with court-Bakufu relations never strayed far from the facts. They never flinched from approaching the fundamental problem, that others governed instead of the Emperor, and

---

Notes to Chapter 10 are found on pages 147-48.

that people would actually fight against the Emperor. This caused progress in the development of historical understanding, up to the point where the rationalism of Arai Hakuseki could make a contribution.

The new aspect of historical understanding that was introduced by *Jinnō Shōtōki*, namely secular historical explanation, became the unquestioned assumption of Arai Hakuseki. We have argued that in *Jinnō Shōtōki* this was the second of three ascending levels of causation: (1) the mystical power of the imperial regalia, (2) the role of institutions governing behaviour, and (3) the will of the Shinto gods.

For Kitabatake, the will of the Shinto gods was the most important causative factor in history. For Arai Hakuseki, the gods did not exist in the way they did for Kitabatake and the people of ancient Japan; thus for him the second level of secular historical explanation was the main level of historical reality. His task was to explain how events led from one stage to another, resulting eventually in the growth of the institutions of his own time, and for this he resorted to the political and military record. This approach marks him as the first "modern" historian of Japan, because modern rational history finds its explanations only in the record of human events and not in the hand of God.

The secularism and pragmatism of Hakuseki's times were a product of the long historical development of the middle ages from the fourteenth to the seventeenth century. With the deepening of military conflict and its spread throughout Japan in the fifteenth and sixteenth centuries, pragmatism came to prevail universally. There was no one who had an ethical or intellectual commitment to national concerns. Universal systems of government, by the court and the Ashikaga Bakufu alike, deteriorated completely, and political power became decentralized among the former officers and vassals of those governments. Under the pressure of continuous civil war, the units of political organization underwent continuous change, resulting in the formation of about 250 independent domains in the mid-sixteenth century. Japan became a collection of kingdoms, with no form of federation beyond transitory military alliances.

In these circumstances there was virtually no concept of a larger purpose for war; imperial house and Ashikaga Bakufu were both completely irrelevant. Surprisingly, both continued to exist. No one took the trouble to extinguish them because they did no apparent harm, until finally Oda Nobunaga (1534-82) chased the last Shogun, Ashikaga Yoshiaki, out of Kyoto in 1573. Hardly anyone noticed.

The regime that Arai Hakuseki served, the Tokugawa Bakufu, was established by conquest at the last great feudal battle at Sekigahara in 1600. Tokugawa Ieyasu (1542-1616) reconstituted the Bakufu as a system of government, taking the title of Shogun in 1603, and set about establishing an institutional basis for the preservation of Tokugawa rule. The measures involved the continuous relocation of the feudal lords (*daimyō*) for security reasons throughout the entire Tokugawa period. The daimyō were also obliged to spend half their time in attendance at the court of the Shogun in the new capital of Edo (present-day Tokyo). This was done according to rosters of attendance, which were carefully drawn up to keep apart potential allies among them. The daimyō were also impoverished because of enforced construction and obligatory travel imposed by the Tokugawa Bakufu. More generally, the physical mobility of all classes of people was restricted, and social mobility was restrained by strict regulation of behaviour according to status. In every respect, the Tokugawa Bakufu showed itself a harsh, vigilant, suspicious regime, with spies everywhere, and cruel punishments for offenders of its strict laws. Dominated by fears for its own security, it even took the extraordinary step of isolating Japan from the world. It expelled the Christian missionaries who had come from Europe in the mid-sixteenth century, ended Japanese trading in East Asia and Southeast Asia, and confined overseas trade to the Dutch and Chinese under severely circumscribed conditions at a single port in Nagasaki.

Such a tyrannical regime was in urgent need of legitimation beyond the right to rule based on conquest; such a basis only invited conquest in turn. Yet the Tokugawa Bakufu itself did not formally establish any theory that advanced beyond the traditional idea of the preceding Kamakura and Ashikaga Bakufu, that the Emperor had delegated his military authority to the Shogun. The Bakufu continued with the ceremonies that embodied this notion. Yet it was clear in early Tokugawa Japan that such a limited theory failed to encompass the new reality of a powerful government claiming complete jurisdiction over every inch of Japanese territory, even though its rule over the feudal domains was indirect. Numerous scholars and officials undertook studies that were related to the problem of legitimacy of the Bakufu, with the bulk of them turning to Confucianism, which thrived from the early seventeenth century throughout the period. It is not surprising that the Tokugawa Bakufu encouraged such studies.[1] Within this general context of scholarly activity related to legitimacy, Arai Hakuseki was the last major figure to continue in the previous tradition of expressing political ideas through historical writing.

Events had run far ahead of the concerns of traditional historical writing. It must have been evident to Hakuseki, as it was not to Kitabatake, that the actions of men from the fourteenth century onward had nothing to do with the imperial house or the imperial state. The imperial regalia were forgotten in the maelstrom of medieval warfare, and the imperial state ceased completely to exist, although there was always a court, however impoverished. The Emperors lived a meagre and fugitive existence, until finally pity was taken on them by Toyotomi Hideyoshi and Tokugawa Ieyasu, who restored them at least to reasonable living conditions. Thus Arai Hakuseki was unencumbered by the idea that the Emperors ought to be a factor in the development of history.

The record also made it plain that there was little observable causative force in history outside of the ambitions and actions of men, their talents and abilities and shortcomings. Added to this was the force of institutions and technologies, as revealed for example in armies and weapons. Perhaps there could also be a type of momentum based on policy and planning, which constituted a factor that came into play upon the realization of other conditions. Such momentum was seen in the building of a military alliance for the ultimate conquest of Japan by the far-sighted Tokugawa Ieyasu. Because of lifelong planning in the service of his own ambition, he became invincible. What we call momentum resembles Hakuseki's *toki no un*, the Force of the Times, which he recognized as a causative factor in history.

This secular view of history was confirmed by Hakuseki's own experience as a high-level bureaucrat in the employ of the Tokugawa Bakufu. He actually began life as a masterless samurai (*rōnin*), until he was employed by the Hotta clan between 1682 and 1691. Hakuseki was a prodigious learner, who was already reading the Confucian classics at the age of four or five, and thus he became renowned for his scholarship. The Kōfu clan next employed him as a lecturer from 1694 on, to instruct Tokugawa Tsunatoyo—who was to become the Shogun Tokugawa Ienobu in 1709.

Hakuseki served as lecturer to the Shogun Ienobu until the death of the latter in 1712. He also served under his successor, Tokugawa Ietsugu, until his death in 1716, and then declined to serve under the next Shogun, Tokugawa Yoshimune. Hakuseki remained out of office until his own death in 1725, devoting his last years to scholarship and producing most of his major works in that period. Undoubtedly his life as a high official in a complicated but effective government confirmed him in a pragmatic view of history. His major involvement was in policy formulation to deal with essentially intractable problems of currency and coinage—a field open more to speculation about policy options and their social consequences than about ethical values. He also knew of intrigue and disappointment. After the death of Tokugawa Ietsugu, the Bakufu Confucianist Hayashi Nobuatsu (1644-1731) became active against Hakuseki, who lost his official residence and became embittered. Harold Bolitho suggests that he deserved it, describing Hakuseki as "jealous, fearful of competition, censorious, opinionated, nitpicking, and aggressively argumentative; to make it worse, he was smart, ambitious, and energetic with it."[2]

Rationalism

We have suggested that history itself, together with Hakuseki's experience in government work, confirmed him in a rational and secular view of history. A second factor disposing him towards this view was his rational position in metaphysics. This was primarily the result of the Confucian thought of his time, based on Chinese Neo-Confucianism, which viewed history fundamentally as a record of facts. The purpose of compiling the facts into historical works was to demonstrate goodness and badness in rulers, thereby presenting a guide for rulers. Behind this lay an ultimate belief that Heaven countenances the continuing rule of only virtuous rulers, which explains the rise and fall of dynasties in China. Bad rulers fell, by the ordinance of Heaven, to be replaced by good ones. It was believed that this was necessarily demonstrated by an objective and dispassionate review of the events of history; they did not have to "cook" the facts.

This attitude towards the facts of history was transferred to Japan in the late medieval period and came to flourish in the works of Hayashi Razan (1583-1657), a Confucian scholar and intimate of Tokugawa Ieyasu. He received Tokugawa Bakufu patronage to found a hereditary school of Confucian studies in history and philosophy, and began a major work of historical writing, *Honchō Tsugan* (Comprehensive History of Japan). Hayashi Razan customarily receives praise as the originator of rationalist history in Japan, upon which Arai Hakuseki based his work. For example, Yasukawa Minoru writes, "Hayashi Razan is the founder of modern historical scholarship. With Razan it departed from medieval historical scholarship, developing into a learning permeated by a positivistic, rational, and critical spirit."[3] The work is especially distinguished in its approach to ancient history. It does not simply copy the original histories of Japan, *Kojiki* and *Nihon Shoki*, as *Gukanshō* and *Jinnō Shōtōki* had done, but is based on Chinese and Korean sources as well, with the aim of critically evaluating all sources in order to arrive at the facts of history.

Tokugawa-period rationalism was so strong that it influenced even scholars for whom the myths of the Age of the Gods were essential. *Dai Nihon Shi*, produced by the Mito domain, was a major work of loyalist history, and hence it had to be based on the myths of the Age of the Gods. But the sponsor of the work, Tokugawa Mitsukuni (1628-1701), confessed that the myths were difficult to handle. "The matters of the Age of the Gods," he said, "are all strange, and hard to include in the chronicle of Emperor Jinmu." Accordingly, the work did not begin with the Age of the Gods, but with the inauguration of imperial rule by Emperor Jinmu.[4] Asaka Tanpaku (1656-1737), one of the scholars who worked on *Dai Nihon Shi* (a major project, lasting from 1657 to 1906), was even more emphatic. "The matters of the Age of the Gods," said Asaka Tanpaku, "are far-fetched and insignificant, and should be disregarded."[5]

Arai Hakuseki worked within the critical rationalism that informed Tokugawa thought. In his work *Koshitsū* (The Essence of Ancient

History, 1716), he offered a reinterpretation of ancient history that was stunning in its implications. As pointed out by Miyazaki Michio, Hakuseki substantially accepted as accurate the narratives presented by the ancient classics, *Kojiki* and *Nihon Shoji*. But he made a transposition for the purpose of better understanding: the acts recorded were those not of gods, but of men.[6] His respect for the great shrines such as Ise and Atsuta was not thereby diminished in the least, because he sought not to destroy the myths but to find their meaning. His fundamental insight was stated thus: "What are called the gods were human beings" (*kami to wa hito nari*). Hakuseki thought that inexact knowledge of the uses of Chinese characters had brought about a misunderstanding of the way the ancients viewed human heroes. The ancients revered the best men, calling them beautiful, but basing their judgment on the way characters came to be used subsequently, people of later times came to believe that the ancients worshipped gods rather than respecting superior men.[7]

In addition to viewing the ancients as heroes rather than deities, Hakuseki sought to rationalize other aspects of the myths, such as the location of events. The Plain of High Heaven (*Takamagahara*), where the activities of the deities took place, was thought by Hakuseki to be an actual place in Hitachi Province. He devoted much energy to a study of place names through the analysis of language usage, thinking that every myth had a real place of reference in Japan; Katsuta Katsutoshi discusses 19 of Hakuseki's identifications. Similarly, Hakuseki rationalized the acts of the gods, suggesting for example that the tales of the birth of the land were myths representing the historic act of the opening of agricultural land by people of ancient times.[8]

His method, which is called euhemerism, had profound significance in two respects. First, he was free to devise a completely new system of periodization. *Kojiki* and *Nihon Shoki* had first introduced the concept of periodization into an Age of the Gods and an Age of Human Emperors. Subsequently no historian prior to Arai Hakuseki, including the Hayashi scholars, had been able to conceptualize the history of Japan in another way. All of them worked with the belief that there had been a wondrous time at the beginning of history, in which fundamental principles were laid down for Japan, involving nation, Emperors, and the people. For Hakuseki, however, there was no divine realm, and no Age of the Gods, but only the history of the Japanese people. The periods he came to devise were based on the location of political power, as we shall see. Second, Hakuseki did not recognize the will of the gods as a factor in historical causation. In *Gukanshō* the importance of the Shinto gods was recognized, and in *Jinnō Shōtōki* their role was overwhelming, as they were announced as the most important cause in history. Since for Arai Hakuseki the gods did not exist as living forces in the way they did for Kitabatake, he necessarily had recourse to another

kind of historical explanation. We have described this as secular historical explanation.

Tokushi Yoron

The most important of Hakuseki's writings is *Tokushi Yoron*, which
arose from his work as lecturer to Tokugawa Ienobu, both before and
after he took office as Shogun. Hakuseki kept careful records of his own
activities, and noted that he lectured on a total of 1,299 occasions over 19
years.

In addition to learning the way of the sages, Tokugawa Ienobu also
had a keen desire to learn the history of Japan, and hence came about
Hakuseki's *Tokushi Yoron*, composed for the purpose of these lectures.
It was completed in the autumn of 1712, but he revised it later in life, with
the final version reaching completion in 1724.[9] This was long after the
occasion of the lectures, so it is clear that the work had assumed the
status in his mind of an independent study of history. However, it
retained the form of a compilation of materials together with commentary. The style is mixed Japanese and Classical Chinese, since he quoted
extensively from other works and left their language intact. (Yasukawa
Minoru also suggests that Classical Chinese was the original form of
Hakuseki's own writing, and that he later put most of it into Japanese.)[10]

Tokushi Yoron is the first work of "modern" scholarship, in the sense
that it is based on a wide range of previous historical writings. It did not
simply present its own viewpoint, and for the most part it acknowledges
quotations and paraphrases from other works. More than 40 works are
explicitly named as sources, and some are relied on to a very great
extent. Since his coverage started in 858, most of the Six National
Histories were not relevant, and he referred only once to *Nihon Montoku Tennō Jitsuroku*, and twice to *Nihon Sandai Jitsuroku*. He preferred such anecdotal works as *Kojidan* (Discussion of Ancient Matters), an early-thirteenth-century mixture of stories and legends by
Minamoto Akikane, and *Gōdanshō* (Miscellaneous Chats of Ōe
Masafusa). He also showed a great liking for *Jinnō Shōtōki*, from which
there are more than 35 quotations. Diaries such as Kujō Kanezane's
Gyokuyō are used, as well as the Historical Tales. Numerous War Tales
are also relied on for their respective periods of history.

Hakuseki also displayed a critical spirit by evaluating the reliability of
his sources, thus deviating from the Chinese tradition of complete
respect for written documents. For example, he relied on *Azuma
Kagami* (Mirror of the East), a document-based history of the Kamakura Bakufu composed probably in the late thirteenth century.
Hakuseki copied great portions of *Azuma Kagami* into his text, but he
noted of one incident, where Hōjō Yoshitoki is assigned the blame for

two murders, "The account written in *Azuma Kagami* is unreliable."[11] However, recent study has shown that this "modern" scholarship of Arai Hakuseki was far from being completely developed. He relied heavily on Hayashi Gahō's *Nihon Ōdai Ichiran* (Survey of the Sovereigns of Japan), but did not acknowledge the full extent of his borrowing.[12]

This imperfection is outweighed, however, by the originality of Hakuseki's approach to history. Freed from dealing with the Age of the Gods, he was able to proceed directly to what he perceived as important. *Jinnō Shōtōki* begins with a declaration of its thesis: "Japan is a divine country." *Tokushi Yoron* also opens with a statement of the thesis that governs the work: "In the government of the realm of Japan there have been nine stages leading to the age of the military houses. There have also been five stages of the military houses, extending to the present age."[13] Citing *Jinnō Shōtōki*, he defines as ancient history the period before Emperor Kōkō (r. 884-887), and begins the analysis with the Ninna era (885-889). The periodization of subsequent history is based on shifts of political power at the imperial court, as follows:

Stage 1 858-872	In the reign of Emperor Seiwa, the Fujiwara Regency is established for a minor Emperor.
Stage 2 876-967	Fujiwara Mototsune deposes Emperor Yōzei, enthrones Emperor Kōkō, and establishes the Fujiwara Regency for adult Emperors.
Stage 3 967-1068	Fujiwara wield power in the reigns of eight Emperors, from Emperor Reizei to Emperor Go Reizei.
Stage 4 1068-86	Emperor Go Sanjō and Emperor Shirakawa rule as Emperors.
Stage 5 1086-1185	Government by Retired Emperors for nine reigns from Emperor Horikawa to Emperor Antoku.

Upon reaching the reign of Emperor Go Toba, the history of political power at the court is overlapped by that of the Bakufu:

Imperial History		Military History	
Stage 6 1185-1219	The Kamakura Shogun assumes power.	Stage 1 1185-1219	Minamoto Yoritomo and two sons rule as Shogun.
Stage 7 1219-1333	Hōjō Regents wield power for 12 reigns, from Emperor Go Horikawa to Emperor Kōgon.	Stage 2 1219-1333	Hōjō Yoshitoki assumes power; Hōjō Regents govern for nine generations.
Stage 8 1333-36	Imperial restoration of Emperor Go Daigo.		

Stage 9 1336-	The Emperors flee. Ashikaga Takauji sets up rival line. Age of warrior rule begins.	Stage 3	The Ashikaga Bakufu assumes power.
		Stage 4	Oda Nobunaga and Toyotomi Hideyoshi govern the realm.
		Stage 5	The present (Tokugawa) era.

In the presentation above, Hakuseki's periodization of history is not very striking. This is because it has the virtue of all brilliant and original ideas: it seems simple and obvious to those who come later. His periodization is a plain recognition of the fact that political power passed from hand to hand. In one time it was held by Emperors, then by Regents, then in another time by Shoguns, and in yet another by Regents for Shoguns, until finally it passed into the hands of the Tokugawa—the auspicious culmination of all historical development. Yet the achievement of Hakuseki was great. First, it is infinitely more intelligible than the murky and involved periodization of *Gukanshō*, which introduced seven stages based on different, poorly defined Principles. Hakuseki's periodization is based on a clear analysis of a single phenomenon, that is, the transformation of political power. Second, it finally solved the problem of imperial history by focusing on the transitions of power instead of on the theory of imperial rule. Arai Hakuseki did not ask why Heaven could allow Emperors to be defeated and exiled. He pointed instead to the historical fact, incontrovertible and undeniable, that the Hōjō family held the power to execute such a decision as the exile of three retired Emperors and the dethronement of the reigning Emperor Chūkyō. He recognized the reality of the historical situation without having his mind hobbled by the values of the ancient system.[14]

Of course Arai Hakuseki, lecturing to the Shogun Tokugawa Ienobu, was an establishment scholar (*goyō gakusha*). Inevitably, therefore, his analysis would demonstrate how the Tokugawa came rightfully to their position of rule. As Ishida Takeshi points out, this was another reason why he liked *Jinnō Shōtōki*: it accepted the institution of the Bakufu as historically valid.[15] Thus it seems that his nine stages of imperial rule constitute a chronicle of decline of imperial power, whereas the five stages of military rule are a tale of glorious rise of the new rulers of Japan, as suggested by Nakamura Kōya.[16] But Miyazaki Michio argues that Part I of *Tokushi Yoron*, chronicling the nine stages of imperial rule, is of equal importance with Parts II and III, which describe the ascendancy of the warriors.[17] This impartial division of history seems to be supported by Hakuseki's apparent respect for the imperial house, as shown in his terminology. He showed a preference for words indicating the imperial nature of Japan. Kurita Mototsugu points out that he used "Our Imperial Court" (*honchō*) instead of "Japan" (*Nihon*); for the court he used "The Heavenly Court" (*tenchō*) rather than "The Court" (*chōtei*); for "Emperor" he used "The Son of Heaven" (*tenshi*) rather than "The Emperor" (*tennō*); for the capital city he used "The Imperial Capital" (*kōkyo*) rather than "The Capital" (*kyōto*).[18] This suggests that Hakuseki was not rushing through the period of imperial history in order to get to his own times. Instead he adopted a dispassionate position about the movement of political power from one institution to another, for both of which he held respect.

Moral Causation and the Force of the Times

There had to be a point to the historical development of Japan as perceived by Arai Hakuseki. Political power did not move aimlessly from the strong to the stronger, but followed the orderly moral rules of the universe. In the end he adhered to conventional Confucian morals, holding that power eventually passed to the most righteous. Only those who could exercise virtuous government obtained the approval of Heaven. For Hakuseki the ultimate causative force in history was the character of the sovereign. As put by Katsuta Katsutoshi, "History according to Arai Hakuseki develops according to who holds supreme political power, and the character of the sovereign power—especially with respect to virtue and wickedness—is the moving force of history."[19] This applied equally to Emperors and military rulers.

Having denied the super-human nature of the deities of ancient Japan, Hakuseki thereby robbed the Emperors of any special dispensation on account of their divine origins. This made them subject to the same necessity to conduct virtuous government as the Shoguns. Put to the test, the Emperors failed, and therefore power inevitably passed from their hands. "One cannot say," writes Hakuseki, "that Emperor Go Toba exercised virtuous government."[20] Emperor Go Daigo also failed: "Emperor Go Daigo was lacking in virtue. Thus when the time came to destroy the Hōjō, despite his repeated attempts to establish a restoration of the imperial government, the empire fell into disorder."[21]

This notion of moral causation is entirely unsupported by the record of history except in the eyes of those who already believe it. Instead, it answers a powerful emotional need to find meaning in history. If Arai Hakuseki had presented only a factual record of political power, without moral interpretation, he would likely be reviled for Machiavellianism rather than praised as an innovative historian. Yet there are some signs that he was indeed Machiavellian. His secular understanding of political processes sometimes undermined his own moral interpretation. For example, Hakuseki adopted *Jinnō Shōtōki* as his major source, but he disagreed with its moral interpretations at some points. He explicitly refuted the view that the rise to power of Minamoto Yoritomo occurred in order to assist the Emperor and succor the people of Japan. In his eyes, it was sufficient to observe that Minamoto Yoritomo arose to fight his enemies and seek power.[22] He also agreed that Hōjō Yoshitoki was a murderous villain, but could not deny that Yoshitoki achieved political success. He recognized that success was equally based on a shrewd practicality that allowed even a blackguard to flourish. He regarded Hōjō Yoshitoki as worse than Soga Umako, who assassinated Emperor Sushun,[23] yet he acknowledged his achievement:

> Yoshitoki exiled three Retired Emperors and two imperial princes and banished an Emperor. He killed two sons of Minamoto Yoriie, a younger brother and a niece of Yoritomo, and he had Kugyō kill Minamoto Sanetomo. His crimes exceeded those of his father Tokimasa. The reason why the warriors of the country followed him was that after the Jōkyū War he seized many properties, and divided them among meritorious fellows, while keeping not a single property for himself.[24]

In order to save his moral interpretation of history against these unwelcome examples, Hakuseki made a necessary adjustment. Creatively, he introduced a notion of the Force of the Times (*toki no un*) to account for such anomalies in history. Because of the Force of the Times, it could happen that a virtuous ruler might appear, but be unable single-handedly to reverse the processes already in motion that were leading to rack and ruin. Hakuseki recognized this in the case of the Shogun Ashikaga Yoshihisa (1465-89), whom he admired for both civil and military accomplishments. He described the Shogun as virtuous, and noted his literary accomplishments.

A poet himself, Ashikaga Yoshihisa sponsored poetry gatherings. In addition he supported lectures on *Nihon Shoki*, and on Chinese classics such as the *Analects of Confucius*, the *Classic of Filial Piety*, and the *Spring and Autumn Annals*. Despite his virtue and his civil and military prowess, however, the time of his rule was one of complete disorder. Ashikaga Yoshihisa became Shogun in 1472, in the midst of the Ōnin War, the worst civil war ever witnessed in Kyoto. Lasting from 1467 to 1477, it was a power struggle between two warlords, Yamana Sōzen and Hosokawa Katsumoto, and in the course of the war most of Kyoto was burnt to the ground. It marked the final stage of the old Heian capital, and the end of pretence of command by the Ashikaga Bakufu. It was fought before the eyes of the Shoguns, and they were powerless to stop it, or even to affect the outcome. Eventually the war was engulfed in the generalized fighting that spread over Japan throughout the succeeding century and a half. Hakuseki explicitly notes the failure of Ashikaga Yoshihisa's virtue to cure the disorder of his times. However, he finds refuge in the *Analects of Confucius*, to which he refers, saying, "Even though there were good men in Yin, King Zhou brought the country to ruin.'' In this passage Confucius comments on the bad last ruler of the Yin dynasty (1523-1028 B.C.?), who caused the lord of Wei to flee, enslaved the lord of Ji, and killed Bigan for offering censure.[25] Such were the times that the three virtuous men were incapable of overcoming the unvirtuous ruler.

Conversely, the Force of the Times explained the otherwise dumb-founding success of apparently unworthy men. Such was the case of Toyotomi Hideyoshi, a peasant who rose to become the conqueror and ruler of all Japan, and thus was unworthy by definition in Confucian social terms. Hakuseki says,

> This man, who rose from rustic origins to rule the empire, is still admired by people, because such a thing is rare in our country. Other countries are not without similar cases. Was it not the case that he simply rode upon the Force of the Times? By this I mean that at the time the empire was filled with traitors and rebels. It was a time when people were respected for bravery and ability in the service of fraud and nothing more, and such things as benevolence, justice, loyalty, and filial piety were unknown. It can be said that Hideyoshi rode upon those times.[26]

Both the concept of Heaven, which approves virtue, and the Force of the Times, which compensates for temporary loss of interest on the part of Heaven, remained vague in Hakuseki's thought. He had no interest at all in metaphysics, and accepted whatever his contemporaries thought Heaven was. Thus he could not explain in detail how Heaven actually functioned to reward the virtuous, or why it sometimes seemed to suffer from a lack of attention to human events. He was equally vague about the Force of the Times, however original the idea. It was a secondary idea in any case, being introduced to rescue morality in history, and perhaps Hakuseki had little to gain by dwelling upon it.

In summary, Arai Hakuseki wrote the first history of Japan that passes with equanimity among rationalist scholars, although it must be admitted that it is an exceedingly boring narrative, thick with names and titles. With *Jinnō Shōtōki* the Japanese tradition of historical writing had developed to the stage of secular historical explanation, in which attention is given to such fundamental matters as economics and political institutions. Secular historical explanation was almost inadvertent in *Jinnō Shōtōki*, but it was primary in Hakuseki's *Tokushi Yoron*. Probably it emerged as central for Hakuseki because of the additional influence of his Neo-Confucian training. Neo-Confucianism encouraged investigation of the myriad things of the world, and this included a rational approach to history.

With the double armour of the Japanese historiographical tradition and Neo-Confucian philosophy, Arai Hakuseki fearlessly approached the gods of ancient Japan. They melted away harmlessly into human inventions. This left Hakuseki free to think about who held political power at a given time, and he concluded that there were nine stages of imperial history and five stages of military history. If we were to study those periods, we might divide history differently from Hakuseki, for example into three stages and seven stages, or some other arrangement—especially after learning that Hakuseki may have adopted the numbers nine and five because of their importance in the Book of Changes.[27] But the originality and validity of his view would not be upset by this; *Tokushi Yoron* still stands as an original and persuasive interpretation of the political history of Japan.

CONCLUSION

Arai Hakuseki brought Japanese political thought in historical writing to its height of development in the traditional period. But there were weaknesses in his thought, which became more apparent after his time. Hakuseki's legitimation of the Bakufu was entirely historical, and not theoretical. Eventually the Bakufu fell, in the middle of the nineteenth century, to forces inspired once more by the idea of imperial restoration, that is, to forces claiming that the Emperor had a superior claim to legitimacy. What was so obvious to Hakuseki, the historical justification of the Bakufu, turned out to have no validity at all. It was clear that the Tokugawa Bakufu had no intellectual resources to respond to the pressures that began to grow against it in the nineteenth century. It is remarkable that a government so powerful and long-established had such little hold on the minds of men, and fell so easily.

The weakness of Hakuseki's thought was partly a general weakness of Japanese Confucianism. Thousands of scholars laboured over the texts for 250 years, with the encouragement of the Bakufu, in the general belief that their work supported the regime. But Confucianism never investigated the variety of political forms, and never doubted the worth of the existing form, whatever it was. Instead it emphasized behaviour within the system, and scholars found endless ways to describe the necessity for observation of the five hierarchical social relationships, with particular emphasis on the need for unquestioning submission to rulers and parents. In response to a powerful demand that unquestioning submission be made to the Emperor instead of the Shogun, Confucianism had nothing to say.

Notes to the Conclusion are found on page 148.

The particular weakness of Hakuseki's thought was the result of the long tradition of Japanese political thinking that we have been examining. We have presented Hakuseki as the culmination of the tradition that began with *Kojiki* and *Nihon Shoki*. They started it with a brilliantly presented historical narrative of the gods, Emperors, and families of Japan. They accomplished the purpose of stating the political ideas of the new imperial government, and they did it so convincingly that no one before Hakuseki was able to conceive of another framework for history. The next groups to rise to power, the Fujiwara Regents and the military clans, had their say, tacking themselves onto the system in Historical Tales and War Tales. Problems and contradictions of the middle ages were examined by direct political analysis, especially *Myōe Shōnin Denki*, but this proved not to be a fresh direction in Japanese political thought. Instead the intellectuals returned to history. Thoughtful works were produced, and we see a steady ascendancy from *Gukanshō* to *Jinnō Shōtōki* to *Tokushi Yoron*. In these terms, Arai Hakuseki represents the height of development within the Japanese tradition of political thought expressed in history. With him the discussion of history became secular and rational, and thus with Hakuseki Japan entered the modern age, which is distinguished by rationalism and differentiation in intellectual endeavour. Hakuseki also fastened upon the location of political power as the prime fact of history, and made it, and not the will of the gods, into the basis for periodization. These were important achievements for the Japanese tradition of political thought. Yet they were not enough.

Arai Hakuseki was unable to develop a taxonomy of political forms, like the Greeks, and to show how one form can turn into another. The Roman historian Polybius was able to argue for the virtue of the Roman constitution precisely because of his understanding of the forms of government and the causes of political change:

> There are six kinds of government, the three mentioned above which are in everybody's mouth (kingship, aristocracy, and democracy) and the three which are naturally allied to them, I mean monarchy, oligarchy, and mob-rule. Now the first of these to come into being is monarchy, its growth being natural and unaided; and next arises kingship derived from monarchy by the aid of art and by the correction of defects. Monarchy first changes into its vicious form, tyranny; and next the abolishment of both gives birth to aristocracy. Aristocracy by its very nature degenerates into oligarchy; and when the commons inflamed by anger takes vengeance on this government for its unjust rule, democracy comes into being; and in due course the licence and lawlessness of this form of government produces mob-rule to complete the series. *The truth of what I have just said will be quite clear to anyone who pays due attention to such beginnings, origins, and changes as are in each case natural. For he alone who has seen how each form naturally arises and develops will be able to see when, how, and where the growth, perfection, change, and end of each are likely*

to occur. And it is to the Roman constitution above all that this method, I think, may be successfully applied, since from the outset its formation and growth have been due to natural causes.[1]

Such a discussion was not possible for Arai Hakuseki. For him, the imperial system had once existed, legitimately; now the Bakufu system existed, legitimately. There was nothing more. He could not classify either of them as a type, arising out of natural causes. Ronald P. Toby has shown that Hakuseki was perfectly clear on the meaning of the terms Emperor and Shogun, and of King (*kokuō*) and Great Prince of Japan (*Nihon koku taikun*) as applied to the Shogun. In his capacity as an official of the Bakufu, Hakuseki tried to manipulate these terms to elevate the status of the Shogun with respect to the rulers of China and Korea.[2] However, in doing so he worked entirely within an established system of meaning with reference to East Asian international relations. His primary purpose as a Confucian was to be certain that each term was correctly applied to its referent. Emperor, Shogun, and King did not signify different types of government to him; they were only names to be used with reference to specific existing governments, in order to rank them correctly.

Without awareness of a variety of possible political forms, Hakuseki was unable to demonstrate a necessary movement from imperial institution to Bakufu. He was not able to argue like Polybius that anyone, by paying attention, could see clearly how Japan got from imperial rule to shogunal rule. The imperial loyalists of the nineteenth century said in effect that there was no necessary development, and that Japan had better return to government by Emperors. Nor, in the end, was Hakuseki able to make normative statements to the effect that the Bakufu possessed peculiar strengths and peculiar excellence for the kind of society in which it existed. Beyond citing historical fact—the Bakufu had indeed come into being—and tendentious virtue—the founder, Tokugawa Ieyasu was morally unsurpassed, which was nothing more than conventional rhetoric—he was essentially unable to explain why the Bakufu was appropriate to society. Thus at the last the limitations of the Japanese tradition of political thought in historical writing became clear.

With the rise of the Confucian philosophy of the Tokugawa period, historical writing ceased to be the main vehicle for expression of political ideas in Japan, and this study properly comes to a conclusion. Confucianism in turn provoked the rise of National Studies (*kokugaku*), thus broadening the range of discussion. It was National Studies, especially as put forth in the writings of Motoori Norinaga (1730-1801), that became the intellectual basis for the modern nationalist movement that swept away the Tokugawa Bakufu, restored the Emperors to sovereignty in the Meiji Restoration of 1868, and launched Japan on its twentieth-century nationalistic development. National Studies concentrated precisely on the ideas put forth in *Kojiki* and *Nihon Shoki* as the foundation of the imperial system: the divine origins of Japan, the founding of the imperial line by the Sun Goddess, the special character of the Japanese people. Their formulations proved to have remarkable staying power, as such ideas became the basis of constitutional law, in which the divinely protected line of Emperors was announced as the sovereign of Japan in the Constitution of 1889, according to which the Emperor is "sacred and inviolable." As the twentieth century progressed and Japan's leaders felt more threatened by the outside world, rationalism in historical and political studies was suppressed in favour of jingoistic incantation of the sacred nature of Japan. In 1940 the scientifically trained historians of Japan's imperial universities hid their reservations and repeated the inauguration of imperial rule by Emperor Jinmu in 660 B. C. as certain fact, on the occasion of the 2,600th anniversary of the event.

However, as we have seen, the Japanese tradition of historical writing did not only provide the ingredients for nationalism, in the form of unshakeable beliefs about the origins of Japan and the imperial house. In the course of its development, the tradition of historical writing generated three great works in *Gukanshō*, *Jinnō Shōtōki*, and *Tokushi Yoron*, which introduced secular historical explanation, and with Arai Hakuseki came rationalism and complete secularism. Hakuseki's style of rationalism was suppressed in twentieth-century Japan until 1945. However, the fact that it had once been independently generated by Japanese was an important underlying factor in the general development of rationalist social studies as the norm in Japan from 1945 to the present.

Historical writing in the nineteenth and twentieth centuries was no longer the primary mode of political discussion, but history played a powerful role in modern Japanese ideology. In a succeeding volume we will take up the development of modern historical writing, and document a range of responses by Japanese historians to the nationalistic purposes of their society.

APPENDICES

APPENDIX A

Reign Dates of Emperors to the Time of Arai Hakuseki

1	Jinmu	660-585 B.C.	20	Ankō	453-456
2	Suizei	581-549	21	Yūryaku	456-479
3	Annei	549-511	22	Seinei	480-484
4	Itoku	510-477	23	Kenzō	485-487
5	Koshō	475-393	24	Ninken	488-498
6	Kōan	392-291	25	Buretsu	498-506
7	Kōrei	290-215	26	Keitai	507-531
8	Kogen	214-158	27	Ankan	531-535
9	Kaika	158-98	28	Senka	535-539
10	Sujin	97-30	29	Kinmei	539-571
11	Suinin	29 B.C.- 70 A.D.	30	Bidatsu	572-585
			31	Yōmei	585-587
12	Keikō	71-130	32	Sushun	587-592
13	Seimu	131-190	33	Suiko ♀	592-628
14	Chūai	192-200	34	Jomei	629-641
	Jingū Kōgō, Regent ♀	201-269	35	Kōgyoku ♀	642-645
15	Ōjin	270-310	36	Kōtoku	645-654
16	Nintoku	313-399	37	Saimei ♀	655-661
17	Richū	400-405	38	Tenji	668-671
18	Hanzei	406-410	39	Kōbun	671-672
19	Ingyō	412-453	40	Tenmu	673-686

♀ denotes a female Emperor

41	Jitō ♀	690-697	78	Nijō	1158-1165
42	Monmu	697-707	79	Rokujō	1165-1168
43	Genmei ♀	707-715	80	Takakura	1168-1180
44	Genshō ♀	715-724	81	Antoku	1180-1183
45	Shōmu	724-749	82	Go Toba	1183-1198
46	Kōken ♀	749-758	83	Tsuchimikado	1198-1210
47	Junnin	758-764	84	Juntoku	1210-1221
48	Shōtoku ♀	764-770	85	Chūkyō	1221
49	Kōnin	770-781	86	Go Horikawa	1221-1232
50	Kanmu	781-806	87	Shijō	1232-1242
51	Heizei	806-809	88	Go Saga	1242-1246
52	Saga	809-823	89	Go Fukakusa	1246-1259
53	Junna	823-833	90	Kameyama	1259-1274
54	Ninmyō	833-850	91	Go Uda	1274-1287
55	Montoku	850-858	92	Fushimi	1288-1298
56	Seiwa	858-876	93	Go Fushimi	1298-1301
57	Yōzei	876-884	94	Go Nijō	1301-1308
58	Kōkō	884-887	95	Hanazono	1308-1318
59	Uda	887-897	96	Go Daigo	1318-1339
60	Daigo	897-930	97	Go Murakami	1339-1368
61	Suzaku	930-946	98	Chōkei	1368-1383
62	Murakami	946-967	99	Go Kameyama	1383-1392
63	Reizei	967-979	100	Go Komatsu	1392-1412
64	En'yū	969-984	101	Shōkō	1412-1428
65	Kazan	984-986	102	Go Hanazono	1429-1464
66	Ichijō	986-1011	103	Go Tuchimikado	1465-1500
67	Sanjō	1011-1016	104	Go Kashiwabara	1500-1526
68	Go Ichijō	1016-1036	105	Go Nara	1526-1557
69	Go Suzaku	1036-1045	106	Ōgimachi	1557-1586
70	Go Reizei	1045-1068	107	Go Yōzei	1586-1611
71	Go Sanjō	1068-1072	108	Go Mizuno-o	1611-1629
72	Shirakawa	1072-1086	109	Meishō	1630-1643
73	Horikawa	1086-1107	110	Go Kōmyō	1643-1654
74	Toba	1107-1123	111	Gosai	1656-1663
75	Sutoku	1123-1141	112	Reigen	1663-1687
76	Konoe	1141-1155	113	Higashiyama	1687-1709
77	Go Shirakawa	1155-1158	114	Nakamikado	1710-1735

The 39th Emperor Kōbun, the 47th Emperor Junnin, and the 85th Emperor Chūkyō were declared legitimate sovereigns by a government decree of 1870.

The Northern Dynasty

1 Kōgon	1332-1333	4 Go Kōgon	1353-1371
2 Kōmyō	1337-1348	5 Go En'yū	1374-1382
3 Sukō	1349-1351		

By a Cabinet decision in 1911 the Southern Dynasty was recognized as the legitimate dynasty during the period of the Northern and Southern Courts.

APPENDIX B

Principal Works of Historical Tales

Eiga Monogatari (A Tale of Flowering Fortunes)

A history of the court during the time of Fujiwara Michinaga (966-1027).

Attributed to a court lady, Akazome Emon.

Ōkagami (The Great Mirror)

A history of the court during the time of Fujiwara Michinaga, in dialogue form.

Author unknown. Eleventh century.

Mizukagami (The Water Mirror)

A history of Japan up to Emperor Ninmyō (r. 833-50); mainly a Japanese rendition of *Fusō Ryakki*.

By Nakayama Tadachika (1131-95) or Minamoto Masayori.

Imakagami (Mirror of the Present Day)

A history of the court in the twelfth century.

Author unknown. 1170.

Masukagami (The Clear Mirror)

A history of Japan, centring on the court, from Genpei War to Restoration of Go Daigo.

Attributed to Nijō Yoshimoto (1320-88).

APPENDIX C

Principal Works of War Tales

Masakadoki (Chronicle of Masakado) History of the uprising of Taira Masakado (d. 940). Composed in *kanbun*. Author unknown. Written soon after 940.

Mutsu Waki (Chronicle of Mutsu Province) History of Earlier Nine Years War, 1051-62. Composed in *kanbun*. Author unknown. Written 1062.

Hōgen Monogatari (Tale of the Disturbance in Hōgen) History of the struggle in the capital, 1156. Developed as a recitative work. Author unknown. Early thirteenth century.

Heiji Monogatari (Tale of the Disturbance in Heiji) History of the struggle in the capital, 1159; Taira clan gained power. Developed as a recitative work. Author unknown. Early thirteenth century.

Heike Monogatari (Tale of the Heike) History of the Genpei War, 1180-85. Premier recitative work. Author unknown. Early thirteenth century.

Genpei Seisuiki (Tale of the Rise and Fall of the Genji and the Heike) History of the Genji and Heike. A work for reading. Author unknown. Middle or late Kamakura.

Jōkyūki (Chronicle of the Disturbance in Jōkyū) History of the Jōkyū War, 1221. Mostly factual. Author unknown. Muromachi.

Baishōron (Discourse of the Plums and Pines) History of founding of Muromachi Bakufu by Ashikaga Takauji. Author unknown. Mid-fourteenth century.

Taiheiki (Chronicle of Grand Pacification) History of restoration attempt by Go Daigo. Kojima Hōshi. 1368-75.

Gikeiki (Chronicle of Yoshitsune). Also known as *Hōgan Monogatari*.	Ballad of Minamoto Yoshitsune, focusing on tragic last years.	Author unknown. Early fifteenth century.
Soga Monogatari (Tale of the Soga Brothers)	Revenge by two Soga brothers in late twelfth century. Taken up in Noh plays and ballads.	Author unknown. Early fourteenth century.
Ōninki (Chronicle of the Ōnin War)	Record of the Ōnin War, 1467-77. Mostly factual.	Author unknown. Written soon after 1477.
Shinchō Kōki (Chronicle of Oda Nobunaga)	History of career of Oda Nobunaga. Mostly factual.	Ōta Gyūichi. 1610.
Taikōki (Chronicle of Toyotomi Hideyoshi)	Career of Toyotomi Hideyoshi. High historical value.	Oze Hōan (1564-1640)

NOTES

Introduction

1 Leo Strauss, *What Is Political Philosophy? and Other Studies* (Glencoe, IL: The Free Press, 1959), p. 12.

Chapter 1

1 Donald L. Philippi, trans., *Kojiki* (Princeton, NJ: Princeton University Press; Tokyo: University of Tokyo Press, 1969), p. 42.
2 Ibid.
3 Ibid., p. 43.
4 Tokumitsu Kyūya, *Kojiki Kenkyū Shi* (Tokyo: Kasama Shoin, 1977), pp. 335-69.
5 For up-to-date reviews of *Kojiki* scholarship, see Mitani Ei'ichi, "Kojiki," in *Jidaibetsu Nihon Bungakushi Jiten*, vol. 1 (Tokyo: Yūseidō, 1987), and Kurano Kenji, "Kojiki," in *Shinchō Nihon Bungaku Jiten* (Tokyo: Shinchōsha, 1988).
6 Philippi, *Kojiki*, p. 41.
7 Sakamoto Tarō, *Nihon no Shūshi to Shigaku* (Tokyo: Shibundō, 1980; originally published in 1966), p. 13.
8 Umezawa Isezō, *Kiki Ron* (Tokyo: Sōbunsha, 1978), pp. 81-83.
9 Philippi, *Kojiki*, pp. 303-304.
10 Ibid., pp. 62-63.
11 Ibid., p. 49.
12 Kurano Kenji and Takeda Yūkichi, eds., *Kojiki, Norito*, Nihon Koten Bungaku Taikei, vol. 1 (Tokyo: Iwanami Shoten, 1976), p. 155.
13 *Nihon Rekishi Daijiten* (Tokyo: Kawade Shobō, 1971), vol. 2, p. 427.
14 Philippi, *Kojiki*, pp. 272-73.
15 Ibid., pp. 174-75.
16 Tsuchihashi Yutaka, *Kodai Kayō no Sekai* (Tokyo: Hanawa Shobō, 1968), pp. 161-62.
17 Hirano Kunio, "Hachi-kyū seiki ni okeru Kikajin mibun no saihen," *Rekishigaku Kenkyū*, 292 (September 1964).
18 Seki Akira, *Kikajin* (Tokyo: Shibundō, 1958), and Ueda Masaaki, *Kikajin* (Tokyo: Chūō Kōronsha, 1965).
19 Saeki Arikiyo, *Shinsen Shōjiroku no Kenkyū*, Honbunhen (Tokyo: Yoshikawa Kōbunkan, 1962), pp. 148, 279-332.

20 A few of the more important works are Yamao Yukihisa, *Nihon no Kokka Keisei* (Tokyo: Iwanami Shoten, 1968); Kadowaki Teiji, *Taika Kaishin* (Tokyo: Tokuma Shoten, 1969); Ishimoda Shō, *Nihon no Kodai Kokka* (Tokyo: Iwanami Shoten, 1971); Kitō Kiyoaki, *Nihon no Kodai Kokka no Keisei to Higashi Ajia* (Tokyo: Azekura Shobō, 1976) and *Hakusuki no E* (Tokyo: Kyōikusha, 1981); and Yoshida Takashi, *Ritsuryō Kokka to Kodai no Shakai* (Tokyo: Iwanami Shoten, 1983).

21 Philippi, *Kojiki*, p. 257.

22 Ibid., pp. 262-63.

23 Kuroita Katsumi, ed., *Shintei Zōho Kokushi Taikei*, Vol. 4: *Nihon Sandai Jitsuroku*, Jōgan 3 (861), 11th month, 11th day (Tokyo: Yoshikawa Kōbunkan, 1935), p. 82.

24 Saeki Arikiyo, *Tomo no Yoshio* (Tokyo: Yoshikawa Kōbunkan, 1970), pp. 175-80.

Chapter 2

1 Kuroita Katsumi, ed., *Shintei Zōho Kokushi Taikei*, Vol. 2: *Shoku Nihongi*, Yōrō 4 (720), 4th month, 21st day (Tokyo: Yoshikawa Kōbunkan, 1937), p. 81.

2 W. G. Aston, trans., *Nihongi, Chronicles of Japan from the Earliest Times to A.D. 697* (London: George Allen and Unwin, 1956; originally published in 1896), vol. 2, p. 350.

3 Ishida Ichirō, "Kokka keisei jidai no rekishi shisō," in *Nihon ni okeru Rekishi Shisō no Tendai* (Tokyo: Nihon Shisōshi Kenkyūkai, 1965), p. 13, and "*Gukanshō* to *Jinnō Shōtōki*," in *Kami to Nihon Bunka* (Tokyo: Perikan-sha, 1983), pp. 78-79.

4 Kitayama Shigeo, *Tenmu Chō* (Tokyo: Chūō Kōronsha, 1978), p. 198.

5 *Kuroita Katsumi, ed., Shintei Zōho Kokushi Taikei*, Vol. 2: *Shoku Nihongi*, p. 81.

6 For up-to-date reviews of *Nihon Shoki* scholarship, see Yokota Ken'ichi, "Nihon Shoki," in *Jidaibetsu Nihon Bungakushi Jiten*, vol. 1 (Tokyo: Yūseidō, 1987), and Kojima Noriyuki, "Nihon Shoki," in *Shinchō Nihon Bungaku Jiten* (Tokyo: Shin-chōsha, 1988).

7 Kojima Noriyuki, *Jōdai Nihon Bungaku to Chūgoku Bungaku* (Tokyo: Hanawa Shobō, 1962), vol. 1, pp. 478-79.

8 Ibid.

9 "Naobi no Mitama," in Ōno Susumu, ed., *Motoori Norinaga Zenshū*, vol. 9 (Tokyo: Chikuma Shobō, 1972), pp. 50-51.

10 James Legge, *The Chinese Classics*, vol. 5: *The Ch'un Ts'ew with the Tso Chuen* (Hong Kong: Hong Kong University Press, 1960), p. 45.

11 William Hung, "The T'ang Bureau of Historiography before 708," *Harvard Journal of Asiatic Studies*, 23 (1960-61), 100.

12 Aston, *Nihongi*, vol. 1, p. 131.

13 Sakamoto Tarō, Ienaga Saburō, Inoue Mitsusada, and Ōno Susumu, eds., *Nihon Shoki*, I, Nihon Koten Bungaku Taikei, vol. 67 (Tokyo: Iwanami Shoten, 1967), pp. 212-13.

14 Saeki Arikiyo, *Shinsen Shōjiroku*, Honbunhen, pp. 141-43.

15 See also John S. Brownlee, "Ideological Control in Ancient Japan," *Historical Reflections*, 14, 1 (1987).

16 Yamada Hideo, *Nihon Shoki* (Tokyo: Kyōikusha, 1979), chart, p. 69.

17 Ibid., p. 67.

18 Sakamoto Tarō, *Nihon no Shūshi to Shigaku*, pp. 6-7.

19 Nakamura Naokatsu, *Kitabatake Chikafusa* (Tokyo: Hokkai Shuppansha, 1937), pp. 5, 115.

Chapter 3

1 Osamu Shimizu, "*Nihon Montoku Tennō Jitsuroku*: An Annotated Translation with a Survey of the Early Ninth Century in Japan" (unpublished Ph.D. thesis, Columbia University, 1951), p. 25.

2 Kojima Noriyuki, *Jōdai Nihon Bungaku to Chūgoku Bungaku*, vol. 1, pp. 478-79.

3 Sakamoto Tarō, *Nihon no Shūshi to Shigaku*, pp. 41-44.

4 Yasko Nishimura, "The Role of Poetry in Japanese Historical Writing: The *Rikkokushi* (unpublished Ph.D. thesis, University of Toronto, 1982), p. 145.
5 Sakamoto Tarō, *Rikkokushi* (Tokyo: Yoshikawa Kōbunkan, 1970), p. 289.
6 Kuroita Katsumi, ed., *Shintei Zōho Kokushi Taikei*, Vol. 3: *Nihon Kōki, Shoku Nihon Kōki, Nihon Montoku Tennō Jitsuroku* (Tokyo: Yoshikawa Kōbunkan, 1937), p. 1.

Chapter 4

1 Matsumoto Haruhisa, "Rekishi Monogatari no sekai," in Ikeda Takeo, ed., *Heianchō Bungaku no Shomondai* (Tokyo: Kasama Shoin, 1977), p. 220.
2 William H. McCullough and Helen Craig McCullough, trans., *A Tale of Flowering Fortunes: Annals of Japanese Aristocratic Life in the Heian Period* (Stanford, CA: Stanford University Press, 1980), vol. 1, p. 69.
3 Ibid., pp. 69-70.
4 Ivan Morris, *The World of the Shining Prince: Court Life in Ancient Japan* (London: Oxford University Press, 1964), pp. 60-61.
5 G. Cameron Hurst III, "Michinaga's Maladies: A Medical History of Fujiwara no Michinaga," *Monumenta Nipponica*, 34, 1 (Spring 1979), 106.
6 McCullough and McCullough, *A Tale of Flowering Fortunes*, vol. 2, p. 673.
7 Ibid., vol. 1, p. 138.
8 Kawakita Noboru, *Eiga Monogatari Kenkyū* (Tokyo: Ōfūsha, 1968), pp. 43-46.
9 Imai Gen'e, *Kazan-in no Shōgai* (Tokyo: Ōfūsha, 1968), pp. 54-64.
10 McCullough and McCullough, *A Tale of Flowering Fortunes*, vol. 1, pp. 192-94.
11 Saeki Umetomo, ed., *Kokin Wakashū*, Nihon Koten Bungaku Taikei, vol. 8 (Tokyo: Iwanami Shoten, 1958), p. 143.
12 "Ōeyama," in Matsushita Daizaburō, ed., *Kokka Taikan* (Tokyo: Kyōbunsha, 1922), p. 235.
13 Helen Craig McCullough, trans., *Ōkagami, The Great Mirror: Fujiwara Michinaga (966-1027) and His Times* (Princeton, NJ: Princeton University Press; Tokyo: University of Tokyo Press, 1980), p. 143.
14 Ibid., p. 91.
15 Ibid., p. 68.
16 Miura Osamu, ed., *Mizukagami, Ōkagami, Masukagami* (Tokyo: Yūhōdō Shoten, 1926), pp. 21, 24, 37.
17 Itabashi Rinkō, *Imakagami* (Tokyo: Asahi Shinbunsha, 1957), p. 75.
18 Ibid., p. 156.
19 Kanō Shigefumi, "*Imakagami* no sekai—*Imakagami* no seiji ishiki no shozai to sono kaimei," *Kokugo Kokubun*, 37, 6 (June 1968).
20 Itabashi Rinkō, *Imakagami*, p. 89.
21 Kanō Shigefumi, "*Imakagami* no sekai," pp. 9-12.
22 Itabashi Rinkō, *Imakagami*, p. 364.
23 Taga Munehaya, "*Imakagami* shiron," *Shigaku Zasshi*, 83, 2 (February 1974), 22.
24 Itabashi Rinkō, *Imakagami*, p. 19.

Chapter 5

1 Yamagishi Tokuhei, Takeuchi Rizō, Ienaga Saburō, and Ōsone Shosuke, eds., *Kodai Seiji Shakai Shisō*, Nihon Shisō Taikei, vol. 8 (Tokyo: Iwanami Shoten, 1979), pp. 78-79.
2 Karl Friday ("Teeth and Claws: Provincial Warriors and the Heian Court," *Monumenta Nipponica*, 43, 2 [Summer 1988]) challenges the established view of the rise of the warriors in the vacuum caused by the decline of the military institutions of the imperial government, and argues that change in military institutions resulted from intentional policies of the government, which remained on top of the situation. However, Friday's view arises from examining documents from the centre, and does not take full account of developments in the manors.

3 Okami Masao and Akamatsu Toshihide, eds., *Gukanshō*, Nihon Koten Bungaku Taikei, vol. 86: (Tokyo: Iwanami Shoten, 1967), pp. 98-99.
4 Kuroita Katsumi, ed., *Shintei Zōho Kokushi Taikei*, Vol. 32: *Azuma Kagami*, Part 1, Bunji 1 (1185), 12th month, 6th day (Tokyo: Yoshikawa Kōbunkan, 1935), p. 188.

Chapter 6

1 Masamune Atsuo, ed., *Hōgen Monogatari, Heiji Monogatari, Jōkyūki* (Tokyo: Nihon Koten Zenshū Kankōkai, 1928), pp. 98-99.
2 Helen Craig McCullough, trans., *Yoshitsune, A Fifteenth Century Japanese Chronicle* (Stanford, CA: Stanford University Press, 1966), p. 123.
3 Kuroita Katsumi, ed., *Shintei Zōho Kokushi Taikei*, Vol. 4: *Nihon Sandai Jitsuroku*, Ninna 2 (886), 4th month, 27th day (Tokyo: Yoshikawa Kōbunkan, 1935), p. 615.
4 Ibid., Ninna 3 (887), 8th month, 17th day, p. 638.
5 McCullough, *Ōkagami*, p. 136.
6 Yamazaki Ken, *Taira no Masakado Seishi* (Tokyo: San'itsu Shobō, 1975), p. 181.
7 Ibid., p. 185.
8 Ibid., p. 183.
9 Ibid.
10 Ibid., p. 192.
11 McCullough, *Ōkagami*, p. 178.
12 Iwasa Masashi, Tokieda Nariki, and Kidō Saizō, eds., *Jinnō Shōtōki, Masukagami*, Nihon Koten Bungaku Taikei, vol. 87 (Tokyo: Iwanami Shoten, 1965), p. 131.
13 William R. Wilson, trans., *Hōgen Monogatari, Tale of the Disorder in Hōgen* (Tokyo: Sophia University Press, 1971), p. 42.
14 A. L. Sadler, trans., "The Heike Monogatari," *Transactions of the Asiatic Society of Japan*, 46, part 1 (1918), 1.
15 Tamagake Hiroyuki, "*Tenshōki* kara *Taikōki* e—Kinseiteki rekishikan no hassei," *Nihon Shisōshi Kenkyū*, 4 (August 1970).

Chapter 7

1 Tamagake Hiroyuki, "Nichiren no rekishikan," *Nihon Shisōshi Kenkyū*, 5 (May 1971), 49-50.
2 Haruyo Lieteau, "The Yasutoki-Myōe Discussion: A Translation from *Togano-o Myōe Shōnin Denki*," *Monumenta Nipponica*, 30, 2 (Summer 1975), 204.
3 Ibid., p. 205.
4 Ibid., p. 207.
5 Kuroita Katsumi, ed., *Shintei Zōho Kokushi Taikei*, Vol. 4: *Nihon Sandai Jitsuroku*, Genkei 7 (883), 11th month, 10th day, p. 544.
6 Kujō Kanezane, *Gyokuyō* (Tokyo: Kokusho Kankōkai, 1906-1907), vol. 1, p. 239.
7 Nezu Masashi, *Tennōke no Rekishi* (Tokyo: San'itsu Shobō, 1973), vol. 1, pp. 197-98.
8 Higo Kazuo et al., *Rekidai Tennō Ki* (Tokyo: Akita Shoten, 1972), p. 243.
9 Iwasa et al., *Jinnō Shōtōki, Masukagami*, pp. 267-68.
10 Ibid., p. 253.
11 G. W. Perkins, "A Study and Partial Translation of *Masukagami*" (unpublished Ph.D. thesis, Stanford University, 1977), p. 159.
12 Iwasa et al., *Jinnō Shōtōki, Masukagami*, p. 279.
13 Perkins, "A Study and Partial Translation of *Masukagami*," p. 166.
14 Iwasa et al., *Jinnō Shōtōki, Masukagami*, p. 279.
15 Inoue Muneo, "*Masukagami* to waka," in Yamagishi Tokuhei and Suzuki Kazuo, eds., *Ōkagami, Masukagami*, Nihon Koten Bungaku, vol. 14 (Tokyo: Kadokawa Shoten, 1977), pp. 369-72.
16 Taya Raishun, "*Masukagami* ni arewareta *Genji Monogatari*," *Kokugo Kokubun*, 4, 10 (October 1934).
17 Kidō Saizō, *Shiron to Rekishi Monogatari*, Kōza Nihon Bungaku, vol. 6: (Tokyo: Zenkoku Daigaku Kokugo Kokubun, 1969), pp. 18-21.

18 S. Uyenaka, "A Study of *Baishōron*: A Source for the Ideology of Imperial Loyalism in Medieval Japan" (unpublished Ph.D. thesis, University of Toronto, 1979), p. 115.
19 Ibid., p. 254.
20 Tamagake Hiroyuki, "*Baishōron* no rekishikan," *Bungei Kenkyū*, 68 (October 1971).
21 Yashiro Kazuo and Kami Hiroshi, *Baishōron Gen'ishū*, Shinsen Nihon Koten Bunko, vol. 3 (Tokyo: Gendai Shinchōsha, 1975), p. 63.
22 Ibid., p. 136.
23 Ibid., p. 41.
24 Ibid., pp. 40-41.
25 Ibid., p. 41.
26 Ibid.
27 Kuroita Katsumi, ed., *Shintei Zōho Kokushi Taikei*, Vol. 32: *Azuma Kagami*, Juei 3 (1184), 2nd month, 25th day, p. 104.
28 Aida Nirō, *Mōko Shūrai no Kenkyū* (Tokyo: Yoshikawa Kōbunkan, 1968), p. 93. The poem is commonly attributed to Ean, but the date of the document is Kōan 8 (1285), subsequent to Ean's death.

Chapter 8

1 Taga Munehaya, *Jien* (Tokyo: Yoshikawa Kōbunkan, 1963), p. 101.
2 Ibid., p. 122.
3 Miura Hiroyuki, "*Gukanshō*," in *Nihonshi no Kenkyū* (Tokyo: Iwanami Shoten, 1922), vol. 1, pp. 1251-57.
4 Delmer M. Brown and Ichirō Ishida, *The Future and the Past. A Translation and Study of the Gukanshō: An Interpretative History of Japan Written in 1219* (Berkeley: University of California Press, 1979), p. 221.
5 Ibid., p. 239.
6 Harada Ryūkichi, "*Gukanshō* no ronri," *Bunka*, 20, 5 (September 1956), 816.
7 Brown and Ishida, *The Future and the Past*, p. 52.
8 Ban Gu, *Han Shu* (Jiulong: Zhonghua Shuju, 1970), Biography of Dong Zhongshu, pp. 1296-97, 2518-19.
9 Brown and Ishida, *The Future and the Past*, p. 19.
10 Ishida Takeshi, "*Gukanshō* to *Jinnō Shōtōki* no rekishi shisō," in Maruyama Masao, ed., *Rekishi Shisōshū* (Tokyo: Chikuma Shobō, 1972), p. 49.
11 Satō Shin'ichi and Ikeuchi Yoshisuke, *Chūsei Hōseishi Shiryōshū* (Tokyo: Iwanami Shoten, 1955), vol. 1, p. 54.
12 Watanabe Tsunaya, ed., *Shasekishū*, Nihon Koten Bungaku Taikei, vol. 85 (Tokyo: Iwanami Shoten, 1966), p. 144.
13 Brown and Ishida, *The Future and the Past*, p. 26.
14 Ibid., pp. 26-27.
15 Ibid., p. 27.
16 Ibid., pp. 206-208.
17 Ibid., p. 182.
18 Akamatsu Toshihide, "Jichin kashō musō ni tsuite," in *Kamakura Bukkyō no Kenkyū* (Kyoto: Heirakuji Shoten, 1957), pp. 267-335.
19 Akamatsu Toshihide, "*Gukanshō* ni tsuite," in *Zoku Kamakura Bukkyō no Kenkyū* (Kyoto: Heirakuji Shoten, 1966), pp. 387-88.

Chapter 9

1 Helen Craig McCullough, trans., *The Taiheiki: A Chronicle of Medieval Japan* (New York: Columbia University Press, 1959), p. 4.
2 Yashiro Kazuo and Kami Hiroshi, *Baishōron Gen'ishū*, p. 65.
3 Satō Shin'ichi, *Nanbokuchō no Dōran*, Nihon no Rekishi, vol. 9 (Tokyo: Chūō Kōronsha, 1965), pp. 70-71.
4 Uyenaka, "A Study of *Baishōron*," p. 142.

5 Ibid., p. 143.
6 Nagahara Keiji, *Jien—Gukanshō; Kitabatake Chikafusa—Jinnō Shōtōki, Shōkan*, Nihon no Meicho, vol. 9 (Tokyo: Chūō Kōronsha, 1971), p. 50.
7 Hirata Toshiharu, *Jinnō Shōtōki no Kisōteki Kenkyū* (Tokyo: Yūzankaku, 1979), chaps. 2 and 4.
8 R. Tsunoda, W. T. de Bary, and Donald Keene, eds., *Sources of Japanese Tradition* (New York: Columbia University Press, 1958), p. 274.
9 Iwasa et al., *Jinnō Shōtōki, Masukagami*, p. 66.
10 Ibid., p. 45.
11 H. Paul Varley, trans., *A Chronicle of Gods and Sovereigns: Jinnō Shōtōki of Kitabatake Chikafusa* (New York: Columbia University Press, 1980), p. 268.
12 Ibid., p. 120.
13 Iwasa et al., *Jinnō Shōtōki, Masukagami*, pp. 177-78.
14 Varley, *A Chronicle of Gods and Sovereigns*, p. 258.
15 Ibid., p. 259.
16 Ibid., p. 219.
17 Iwasa et al., *Jinnō Shōtōki, Masukagami*, p. 185.
18 Varley, *A Chronicle of Gods and Sovereigns*, p. 229.
19 Ibid., pp. 224-25.
20 Iwasa et al., *Jinnō Shōtōki, Masukagami*, p. 180.
21 Ibid., p. 163. The editors of the Nihon Koten Bungaku Taikei edition note that there is a similar passage in *Gochinza Denki*, a Kamakura period work on the origins and history of the Inner and Outer Shrines of Ise, without specifically stating that Kitabatake saw it. Books on Shinto such as this were not widely circulated, but Kitabatake may have had access to it because of his special interest in Shinto. The passage runs, "Humans therefore are Heaven's divine creatures; their spirits must not be harmed" ("Gochinza Denki," in Kuroita Katsumi, ed., *Shintei Zōho Kokushi Taikei*, vol. 7: *Kojiki, Sendai Kuji Hongi, Shintō Gobusho* [Tokyo: Yoshikawa Kōbunkan, 1937], p. 14).
22 Tokutomi Iichirō "Sohō," *The Imperial Rescript Declaring War on United States and British Empire* (Osaka: The Osaka Mainichi; Tokyo: The Tokyo Nichi Nichi, 1942), p. 4.
23 Ibid., pp. 6-8.
24 Nagahara Keiji, *Kōkoku Shikan*, Iwanami Booklet no. 20 (Tokyo: Iwanami Shoten, 1983), pp. 15-18, and Inoue Kiyoshi and Mōri Kōichi, *Yugamerareta Kodaishi* (Tokyo: Asahi Shinbunsha, 1973), pp. 20-22.
25 Hiraizumi Kiyoshi, *Chūsei ni okeru Kokutai Kannen* (Tokyo: Iwanami Shoten, 1933), pp. 58-66.
26 Kojima Yoshio, *Jinnō Shōtōki no Kenkyū* (Tokyo: Iwanami Shoten, 1933), pp. 31-32.

Chapter 10

1 Herman Ooms, *Tokugawa Ideology: Early Constructs, 1570-1680* (Princeton, NJ: Princeton University Press, 1985).
2 Harold Bolitho, review of Kate Wildman Nakai, *Shogunal Politics: Arai Hakuseki and the Premises of Tokugawa Rule*," *Monumenta Nipponica*, 44, 3 (Autumn 1989).
3 Yasukawa Minoru, *Honchō Tsugan no Kenkyū* (Tokyo: Gensōsha, 1980), p. 27.
4 *Yakubun Dai Nihon Shi* (Tokyo: Kokumin Bunko Kankōkai, 1915), vol. 1, p. 2.
5 Ozawa Ei'ichi, *Kindai Nihon Shigakushi no Kenkyū* (Tokyo: Yoshikawa Kōbunkan, 1966-68), Bakumatsu-hen, p. 130.
6 Miyazaki Michio, *Arai Hakuseki Joron* (Tokyo: Yoshikawa Kōbunkan, 1976), pp. 160-61.
7 *Koshitsū*, in Maruyama Masao, ed., *Rekishi Shisōshū* (Tokyo: Chikuma Shobō, 1972), p. 258.
8 Katsuta Katsutoshi, *Arai Hakuseki no Rekishigaku* (Tokyo: Kōseikaku, 1939), pp. 49-54. For further discussion of Hakuseki's handling of the Age of the Gods, see Kate Wildman Nakai, *Shogunal Politics: Arai Hakuseki and the Premises of Tokugawa Rule* (Cambridge, MA: Harvard University Press, 1988), chap. 8.

9 Miyazaki Michio, "*Tokushi Yoron* kō," *Hirosaki Daigaku Jinbun Shakai*, 19 (1965), 5.
10 Yasukawa Minoru, "*Tokushi Yoron* no seiritsu," *Shintōgaku*, 99 (November 1978), 39.
11 Matsumura Akira, Bitō Masahide, and Kato Shūichi, eds., *Arai Hakuseki*, Nihon Shisō Taikei, vol. 35 (Tokyo: Iwanami Shoten, 1975), p. 318.
12 Miyazaki Michio, "Hayashi-ke shigaku to Hakuseki shigaku," *Nihon Rekishi*, 148 (October 1960), 3-5, and Yasukawa, *Honchō Tsugan no Kenkyū*, pp. 236-42.
13 Matsumura et al., *Arai Hakuseki*, p. 184.
14 My reference to the recognition of political power can be put more decorously in terms of the Confucian principle of comprehensive authority by which effective regimes were recognized (Nakai, *Shogunal Politics*, pp. 183-85).
15 Ishida Takeshi, "*Gukanshō* to *Jinnō Shōtōki* no rekishi shisō," in Maruyama, ed., *Rekishi Shisōshū*, pp. 61-62.
16 Nakamura Kōya, "Shika to shite no Arai Hakuseki," in *Honpō Shigakushi Ronsō* (Tokyo: Fuzanbō, 1939), vol. 2, p. 980.
17 Miyazaki Michio, "*Tokushi Yoron* kō," pp. 5-11.
18 Kurita Mototsugu, *Arai Hakuseki no Bunchi Seiji* (Tokyo: Ishizaki Shoten, 1962), p. 580.
19 Katsuta Katsutoshi, *Arai Hakuseki no Gakumon to Shisō* (Tokyo: Yūzankaku, 1973), p. 323.
20 Matsumura et al., *Arai Hakuseki*, p. 275.
21 Ibid.
22 Ibid., pp. 294-95.
23 Ibid., pp. 318-19.
24 Ibid., p. 330.
25 Yoshikawa Kōjirō, *Rongo* (Tokyo: Asahi Shinbunsha, 1966), vol. 2, pp. 288-89.
26 Matsumura et al., *Arai Hakuseki*, p. 429.
27 Ulrich Gogh, "*Tokushi Yoron* ni okeru Jidai Kubun no Bunseki," in Miyazaki Michio, ed., *Arai Hakuseki no Gendaiteki Kōsatsu* (Tokyo: Yoshikawa Kōbunkan, 1985), pp. 185-97.

Conclusion

1 William Ebenstein, *Great Political Thinkers: Plato to the Present* (New York: Holt, Rinehart and Winston, 1969), p. 115 (italics added).
2 Ronald P. Toby, "Korean-Japanese Diplomacy in 1711: Sukchong's Court and the Shōgun's Title," *Chōsen Gakuhō*, 74 (January 1975), 1-26.

BIBLIOGRAPHY

Aida Nirō. *Mōko Shūrai no Kenkyū*. Tokyo: Yoshikawa Kōbunkan, 1968.
Akamatsu Toshihide. *Kamakura Bukkyō no Kenkyū*. Kyoto: Heirakuji Shoten, 1957.
_____. *Zoku Kamakura Bukkyō no Kenkyū*. Kyoto: Heirakuji Shoten, 1966.
Aston, W. G., trans. *Nihongi, Chronicles of Japan from the Earliest Times to A.D. 697*. 2 vols. London: George Allen and Unwin, 1956; originally published in 1896.
Ban Gu. *Han Shu*. Jiulong: Zhonghua Shuju, 1970.
Bolitho, Harold. Review of Kate Wildman Nakai, *Shogunal Politics: Arai Hakuseki and the Premises of Tokugawa Rule*. *Monumenta Nipponica*, 44, 3 (Autumn 1989).
Brown, Delmer M., and Ishida Ichirō. *The Future and the Past. A Translation and Study of the* Gukanshō: *An Interpretative History of Japan Written in 1219*. Berkeley: University of California Press, 1979.
Brownlee, John S. "Ideological Control in Ancient Japan." *Historical Reflections*, 14, 1 (1987).
Ebenstein, William. *Great Political Thinkers: Plato to the Present*. 4th ed. New York: Holt, Rinehart, and Winston, 1969.
Friday, Karl. "Teeth and Claws: Provincial Warriors and the Heian Court." *Monumenta Nipponica*, 43, 2 (Summer 1988).
Gogh, Ulrich. "*Tokushi Yoron* ni okeru Jidai Kubun no Bunseki," in Miyazaki Michio, ed., *Arai Hakuseki no Gendaiteki Kōsatsu*. Tokyo: Yoshikawa Kōbunkan, 1985.
Harada Ryūkichi. "*Gukanshō* no ronri." *Bunka*, 20, 5 (September 1956).
Higo Kazuo, Mitobe Masao, Fukuchi Shigetada, and Akagai Shizuko. *Rekidai Tennō Ki*. Tokyo: Akita Shoten, 1972.
Hiraizumi Kiyoshi. *Chūsei ni okeru Kokutai Kannen*. Tokyo: Iwanami Shoten, 1933.

150

Hirano Kunio. "Hachi-kyū seiki in okeru Kikajin mibun no saihen."
    Rekishigaku Kenkyū, 292 (September 1964).
Hirata Toshiharu. *Jinnō Shōtōki no Kisōteki Kenkyū*. Tokyo: Yūzankaku, 1979.
Hung, William. "The T'ang Bureau of Historiography Before 708." *Harvard
    Journal of Asiatic Studies*, 23 (1960-61).
Hurst, G. Cameron III. "Michinaga's Maladies: A Medical History of Fujiwara
    no Michinaga." *Monumenta Nipponica*, 34, 1 (Spring 1979).
Imai Gen'e. *Kazan-in no Shōgai*. Tokyo: Ōfūsha, 1968.
Inoue Kiyoshi and Mōri Kōichi. *Yugamerareta Kodaishi*. Tokyo: Asahi Shin-
    bunsha, 1973.
Inoue Muneo. "*Masukagami* to waka." In Yamagishi Tokuhei and Suzuki
    Kazuo, eds. *Ōkagami, Masukagami*. Nihon Koten Bungaku, vol. 14.
    Tokyo: Kadokawa Shoten, 1977.
Ishida Ichirō. "*Gukanshō* to *Jinnō Shōtōki*." In *Kami to Nihon Bunka*. Tokyo:
    Perikansha, 1983.
————. "Kokka keisei jidai no rekishi shisō." In *Nihon ni okeru Rekishi
    Shisō no Tenkai*. Tokyo: Nihon Shisōshi Kenkyūkai, 1965.
Ishida Takeshi. "*Gukanshō* to *Jinnō Shōtōki* no rekishi shisō." In Maruyama
    Masao, ed., *Rekishi Shisōshū*. Tokyo: Chikuma Shobō, 1972.
Ishimoda Shō. *Nihon no Kodai Kokka*. Tokyo: Iwanami Shoten, 1971.
Itabashi Rinkō. *Imakagami*. Tokyo: Asahi Shinbunsha, 1957.
Iwasa Masashi, Tokieda Nariki, and Kidō Saizō, eds. *Jinnō Shōtōki,
    Masukagami*. Nihon Koten Bungaku Taikei, vol. 87. Tokyo: Iwanami
    Shoten, 1965.
Kadowaki Teiji. *Taika Kaishin*. Tokyo: Tokuma Shoten, 1969.
Kanō Shigefumi. "*Imakagami* no sekai—*Imakagami* no seiji ishiki no shozai to
    sono kaimei." *Kokugo Kokubun*, 37, 6 (June 1968)
Katsuta Katsutoshi. *Arai Hakuseki no Rekishigaku*. Tokyo: Kōseikaku, 1939.
————. *Arai Hakuseki no Gakumon to Shisō*. Tokyo: Yūzankaku, 1973.
Kawakita Noboru. *Eiga Monogatari Kenkyū*. Tokyo: Ōfūsha, 1968.
Kidō Saizō. *Shiron to Rekishi Monogatari*. Kōza Nihon Bungaku, vol. 6.
    Tokyo: Zenkoku Daigaku Kokugo Kokubun, 1969.
Kitayama Shigeo. *Tenmu Chō*. Tokyo: Chūō Kōronsha, 1978.
Kitō Kiyoaki. *Nihon no Kodai Kokka no Keisei to Higashi Ajia*. Tokyo: Aze-
    kura Shobō, 1976.
————. *Hakusuki no E*. Tokyo: Kyōikusha, 1981.
Kojima Noriyuki. *Jōdai Nihon Bungaku to Chūgoku Bungaku*. 2 vols. Tokyo:
    Hanawa Shobō, 1962.
————. "Nihon Shoki." In *Shinchō Nihon Bungaku Jiten*. Tokyo: Shin-
    chōsha, 1988.
Kojima Yoshio. *Jinnō Shōtōki no Kenkyū*. Tokyo: Iwanami Shoten, 1933.
Kujō Kanezane. *Gyokuyō*. Vol. 1. 3 vols. Tokyo: Kokusho Kankōkai,
    1906-1907.
Kurano Kenji. "Kojiki." In *Shinchō Nihon Bungaku Jiten*. Tokyo: Shinchōsha,
    1988.
———— and Takeda Yūkichi, eds. *Kojiki, Norito*. Nihon Koten Bungaku
    Taikei, vol. 1. Tokyo: Iwanami Shoten 1976.
Kurita Mototsugu. *Arai Hakuseki no Bunchi Seiji*. Tokyo: Ishizaki Shoten,
    1962.

Kuroita Katsumi, ed. *Shintei Zōho Kokushi Taikei*. 60 vols. Tokyo: Yoshikawa Kobunkan, 1934-60.
————. Vol. 2: *Shoku Nihongi*. 1937.
————. Vol. 3: *Nihon Kōki, Shoku Nihon Kōki, Nihon Montoku Tennō Jitsuroku*. 1937.
————. Vol. 4: *Nihon Sandai Jitsuroku*. 1935.
————. Vol. 7: *Kojiki, Sendai Kuji Hongi, Shintō Gobusho*. 1937.
————. Vol. 32: *Azuma Kagami*, Part 1. 1935.
Legge, James. *The Chinese Classics*. Vol. 5: *The Ch'un Ts'ew with the Tso Chuen*. 5 vols. Hong Kong: Hong Kong University Press, 1960.
Lieteau, Haruyo. "The Yasutoki-Myōe Discussion: A Translation from *Togano-o Myōe Shōnin Denki*." *Monumenta Nipponica*, 30, 2 (Summer 1975).
Maruyama Masao, ed. *Rekishi Shisōshū*. Tokyo: Chikuma Shobō, 1972.
Masamune Atsuo, ed. *Hōgen Monogatari, Heiji Monogatari, Jōkyūki*. Tokyo: Nihon Koten Zenshū Kankōkai, 1928.
Matsumoto Haruhisa. "Rekishi Monogatari no sekai." In Ikeda Takeo, ed., *Heianchō Bungaku no Shomondai*. Tokyo: Kasama Shoin, 1977.
Matsumura Akira, Bitō Masahide, and Kato Shūichi, eds. *Arai Hakuseki*. Nihon Shisō Taikei, vol. 35. Tokyo: Iwanami Shoten, 1975.
Matsushita Daizaburō, ed. *Kokka Taikan*. Tokyo: Kyōbunsha, 1922.
McCullough, Helen Craig, trans. *The Taiheiki: A Chronicle of Medieval Japan*. New York: Columbia University Press, 1959.
————, trans. *Ōkagami, The Great Mirror: Fujiwara Michinaga (966-1027) and His Times*. Princeton, NJ: Princeton University Press; Tokyo: University of Tokyo Press, 1980.
————, trans. *Yoshitsune, A Fifteenth Century Japanese Chronicle*. Stanford, CA: Stanford University Press, 1966.
McCullough, William H., and McCullough, Helen Craig, trans. *A Tale of Flowering Fortunes: Annals of Japanese Aristocratic Life in the Heian Period*. 2 vols. Stanford, CA: Stanford University Press, 1980.
Miura Hiroyuki. *Nihonshi no Kenkyū*. 2 vols. Tokyo: Iwanami Shoten, 1922.
Mitani Ei'ichi. "Kojiki." In *Jidaibetsu Nihon Bungakushi Jiten*. Vol. 1. Tokyo: Yūseidō, 1987.
Miura Osamu, ed. *Mizukagami, Ōkagami, Masukagami*. Tokyo: Yūhōdō Shoten, 1926.
Miyazaki Michio. *Arai Hakuseki Joron*. Tokyo: Yoshikawa Kōbunkan, 1976.
————. "Tokushi Yoron kō." *Hirosaki Daigaku Jinbun Shakai*, 19 (1965).
————. "Hayashi-ke shigaku to Hakuseki shigaku." *Nihon Rekishi*, 148 (October 1960).
Morris, Ivan. *The World of the Shining Prince: Court Life in Ancient Japan*. London: Oxford University Press, 1964.
Nagahara Keiji. *Jien—Gukanshō; Kitabatake Chikafusa—Jinnō Shōtōki, Shōkan*. Nihon no Meicho, vol. 9. Tokyo: Chūō Kōronsha, 1971.
————. *Kōkoku Shikan*. Iwanami Booklet no. 20. Tokyo: Iwanami Shoten, 1983.
Nakai, Kate Wildman. *Shogunal Politics: Arai Hakuseki and the Premises of Tokugawa Rule*. Cambridge, MA: Harvard University Press, 1988.

Nakamura Kōya. "Shika to shite no Arai Hakuseki." In *Honpō Shigakushi Ronsō*. Vol. 2. Tokyo: Fuzanbō, 1939.

Nakamura Naokatsu. *Kitabatake Chikafusa*. Tokyo: Hokkai Shuppansha, 1937.

Nezu Masashi. *Tennōke no Rekishi*. 2 vols. Tokyo: San'itsu Shobō, 1973.

Nihon Rekishi Daijiten. Vol. 2. Tokyo: Kawade Shobō, 1971.

Nishimura, Yasko. "The Role of Poetry in Japanese Historical Writing: The *Rikkokushi*." Unpublished Ph.D. thesis, University of Toronto, 1982.

Okami Masao and Akamatsu Toshihide, eds. *Gukanshō*. Nihon Koten Bungaku Taikei, vol. 86. Tokyo: Iwanami Shoten, 1967.

Ōno Susumu, ed. *Motoori Norinaga Zenshū*. Vol. 9. Tokyo: Chikuma Shobō, 1968.

Ooms, Herman. *Tokugawa Ideology: Early Constructs, 1570-1680*. Princeton, NJ: Princeton University Press, 1985.

Ozawa Ei'ichi. *Kindai Nihon Shigakushi no Kenkyū*. 2 vols. Tokyo: Yoshikawa Kōbunkan, 1966-68.

Perkins, G. W. "A Study and Partial Translation of *Masukagami*." Unpublished Ph.D. thesis, Stanford University, 1977.

Philippi, Donald L., trans. *Kojiki*. Princeton, NJ: Princeton University Press; Tokyo: University of Tokyo Press, 1969.

Sadler, A. L., trans. "The Heike Monogatari." *Transactions of the Asiatic Society of Japan*, 46, part 1 (1918).

Saeki Arikiyo. *Tomo no Yoshio*. Tokyo: Yoshikawa Kōbunkan, 1970.

————. *Shinsen Shōjiroku no Kenkyū*, Honbunhen (Tokyo: Yoshikawa Kōbunkan, 1962.

Saeki Umetomo, ed. *Kokin Wakashū*. Nihon Koten Bungaku Taikei, vol. 8. Tokyo: Iwanami Shoten, 1958.

Sakamoto Tarō. *Nihon no Shūshi to Shigaku*. Tokyo: Shibundō, 1980; originally published in 1966.

————. *Rikkokushi*. Tokyo: Yoshikawa Kōbunkan, 1970.

————, Ienaga Saburō, Inoue Mitsusada, and Ōno Susumu, eds. *Nihon Shoki*, I. Nihon Koten Bungaku Taikei, vol. 67. Tokyo: Iwanami Shoten, 1967.

Satō Shin'ichi. *Nanbokuchō no Dōran*. Nihon no Rekishi, vol. 9. Tokyo: Chūō Kōronsha, 1965.

————, and Ikeuchi Yoshisuke. *Chūsei Hōseishi Shiryōshū*. Vol. 1. Tokyo: Iwanami Shoten, 1955.

Seki Akira. *Kikajin*. Tokyo: Shibundō, 1958.

Shimizu, Osamu. "*Nihon Montoku Tennō Jitsuroku*: An Annotated Translation with a Survey of the Early Ninth Century in Japan." Unpublished Ph.D. thesis, Columbia University, 1951.

Strauss, Leo. *What Is Political Philosophy? and Other Studies*. Glencoe, IL: The Free Press, 1959.

Taga Munehaya. *Jien*. Tokyo: Yoshikawa Kōbunkan, 1963.

————. "*Imakagami* shiron." *Shigaku Zasshi*, 83, 2 (February 1974).

Tamagake Hiroyuki. "*Baishōron* no rekishikan." *Bungei Kenkyū*, 68 (October 1971).

————. "Nichiren no rekishikan." *Nihon Shisōshi Kenkyū*, 5 (May 1971).

————. "*Tenshōki* kara *Taikōki* e — Kinseiteki rekishikan no hassei." *Nihon Shisōshi Kenkyū*, 4 (August 1970).
Taya Raishun. "*Masukagami* ni arewareta *Genji Monogatari*." *Kokugo Kokubun*, 4, 10 (October 1934).
Toby, Ronald P. "Korean-Japanese Diplomacy in 1711: Sukchong's Court and the Shōgun's Title." *Chōsen Gakuhō*, 74 (January 1975).
Tokumitsu Kyūya. *Kojiki Kenkyū Shi*. Tokyo: Kasama Shoin, 1977.
Tokutomi Iichirō "Sohō." *The Imperial Rescript Declaring War on United States and British Empire* [*sic*]. Osaka: The Osaka Mainichi; Tokyo: The Tokyo Nichi Nichi, 1942.
Tsuchihashi Yutaka. *Kodai Kayō no Sekai*. Tokyo: Hanawa Shobō, 1968.
Tsunoda, R., W. T. de Bary, and Donald Keene, eds. *Sources of Japanese Tradition*. New York: Columbia University Press, 1958.
Ueda Masaaki. *Kikajin*. Tokyo: Chūō Kōronsha, 1965.
Umezawa Isezō. *Kiki Ron*. Tokyo: Sōbunsha, 1978.
Uyenaka, S. "A Study of *Baishōron*: A Source for the Ideology of Imperial Loyalism in Medieval Japan." Unpublished Ph.D. thesis, University of Toronto, 1979.
Varley, H. Paul, trans. *A Chronicle of Gods and Sovereigns: Jinnō Shōtōki of Kitabatake Chikafusa*. New York: Columbia University Press, 1980.
Watanabe Tsunaya, ed. *Shasekishū*. Nihon Koten Bungaku Taikei, vol. 85. Tokyo: Iwanami Shoten, 1966.
Wilson, William R., trans. *Hōgen Monogatari: Tale of the Disorder in Hōgen*. Tokyo: Sophia University Press, 1971.
Yakubun Dai Nihon Shi. Vol. 1. 5 vols. Tokyo: Kokumin Bunko Kankōkai, 1915.
Yamada Hideo. *Nihon Shoki*. Tokyo: Kyōikusha, 1979.
Yamagishi Tokuhei, Takeuchi Rizō, Ienaga Saburō, and Ōsone Shosuke, eds. *Kodai Seiji Shakai Shisō*. Nihon Shisō Taikei, vol. 8. Tokyo: Iwanami Shoten, 1979.
Yamao Yukihisa. *Nihon no Kokka Keisei*. Tokyo: Iwanami Shoten, 1968.
Yamazaki Ken. *Taira no Masakado Seishi*. Tokyo: San'itsu Shobō, 1975.
Yashiro Kazuo and Kami Hiroshi. *Baishōron Gen'ishū*. Shinsen Nihon Koten Bunko, vol. 3. Tokyo: Gendai Shinchōsha, 1975.
Yasukawa Minoru. *Honchō Tsugan no Kenkyū*. Tokyo: Gensōsha, 1980.
————. "*Tokushi Yoron* no seiritsu." *Shintōgaku*, 99 (November 1978).
Yokota Ken'ichi. "Nihon Shoki." In *Jidaibetsu Nihon Bungakushi Jiten*. Vol. 1. Tokyo: Yūseidō, 1987.
Yoshida Takashi. *Ritsuryō Kokka to Kodai no Shakai*. Tokyo: Iwanami Shoten, 1983.
Yoshikawa Kōjirō. *Rongo*. 2 vols. Tokyo: Asahi Shinbunsha, 1966.

INDEX